OXFORD WORLD'[

ECCE HO

FRIEDRICH NIETZSCHE (1844–1900) was born in Röcken, Saxony, and educated at the universities of Bonn and Leipzig. At the age of only 24 he was appointed Professor of Classical Philology at the University of Basle, but prolonged bouts of ill health forced him to resign from his post in 1879. Over the next decade he shuttled between the Swiss Alps and the Mediterranean coast, devoting himself entirely to thinking and writing. His early books and pamphlets (*The Birth of Tragedy, Untimely Meditations*) were heavily influenced by Wagner and Schopenhauer, but from *Human, All Too Human* (1878) on, his thought began to develop more independently, and he published a series of ground-breaking philosophical works (*The Gay Science, Thus Spoke Zarathustra, Beyond Good and Evil, On the Genealogy of Morals*) which culminated in a frenzy of production in the closing months of 1888. In January 1889 Nietzsche suffered a mental breakdown from which he was never to recover, and he died in Weimar eleven years later. *Ecce Homo* (1888) is a mischievously provocative autobiography, a blasphemous exercise in self-styling in which he reviews his life and work from a 'divine' perspective of absolute affirmation.

DUNCAN LARGE, former Chairman of the Friedrich Nietzsche Society, is Reader in German at Swansea University. He has translated Nietzsche's *Twilight of the Idols* for Oxford World's Classics (1998) and co-edited (with Keith Ansell Pearson) *The Nietzsche Reader* (Blackwell, 2005). He is the author of *Nietzsche and Proust: A Comparative Study* (Oxford University Press, 2001) and is currently completing a monograph on *Nietzsche's Renaissance Figures*.

OXFORD WORLD'S CLASSICS

*For over 100 years Oxford World's Classics have brought
readers closer to the world's great literature. Now with over 700
titles—from the 4,000-year-old myths of Mesopotamia to the
twentieth century's greatest novels—the series makes available
lesser-known as well as celebrated writing.*

*The pocket-sized hardbacks of the early years contained
introductions by Virginia Woolf, T. S. Eliot, Graham Greene,
and other literary figures which enriched the experience of reading.
Today the series is recognized for its fine scholarship and
reliability in texts that span world literature, drama and poetry,
religion, philosophy and politics. Each edition includes perceptive
commentary and essential background information to meet the
changing needs of readers.*

OXFORD WORLD'S CLASSICS

FRIEDRICH NIETZSCHE

Ecce Homo
How To Become What You Are

Translated with an Introduction and Notes by
DUNCAN LARGE

OXFORD
UNIVERSITY PRESS

OXFORD
UNIVERSITY PRESS

Great Clarendon Street, Oxford OX2 6DP

Oxford University Press is a department of the University of Oxford.
It furthers the University's objective of excellence in research, scholarship,
and education by publishing worldwide in

Oxford New York

Auckland Cape Town Dar es Salaam Hong Kong Karachi
Kuala Lumpur Madrid Melbourne Mexico City Nairobi
New Delhi Shanghai Taipei Toronto

With offices in

Argentina Austria Brazil Chile Czech Republic France Greece
Guatemala Hungary Italy Japan Poland Portugal Singapore
South Korea Switzerland Thailand Turkey Ukraine Vietnam

Oxford is a registered trade mark of Oxford University Press
in the UK and in certain other countries

Published in the United States
by Oxford University Press Inc., New York

First published as an Oxford World's Classics paperback 2007
Reissued 2009

British Library Cataloguing in Publication Data

Data available

Library of Congress Cataloging in Publication Data

Nietzsche, Friedrich Wilhelm, 1844–1900.
[Ecce homo. English]
Ecce homo : how to become what you are / Friedrich Nietzsche ; translated
with an introduction and notes by Duncan Large.
p. cm.
Includes bibliographical references and index.
ISBN 978–0–19–955256–6 (alk. paper) .
I. Nietzsche, Friedrich Wilhelm, 1844–1900. 2. Philosopher—Germany—
Biography. I. Large, Duncan. II. Title.
B3316.N34A3413 2007
193–dc21
2006039681

ISBN 978–0–19–955256–6

15

Typeset by Cepha Imaging Private Ltd., Bangalore, India
Printed in Great Britain
on acid-free paper by
Clays Ltd, Elcograf S.p.A.

TO THE MEMORY OF

SARAH KOFMAN

1934–1994

CONTENTS

ABBREVIATIONS

Cross-references within *Ecce Homo* are by chapter and paragraph number, with the chapters referred to in abbreviated form as follows:

F: Foreword
I: Why I Am So Wise
II: Why I Am So Clever
III: Why I Write Such Good Books
IV: Why I Am a Destiny

References to Nietzsche's other works are also by paragraph number, except for the correspondence and the unpublished notes not collected in *The Will to Power*, where volume and page references to the German editions are given. The following are the abbreviations used and the editions from which illustrative quotations have been taken:

AC   *The Antichrist* (1888), in *Twilight of the Idols and The Anti-Christ*, trans. R. J. Hollingdale (Harmondsworth: Penguin, 1968)

BAW   *Friedrich Nietzsche: Frühe Schriften*, ed. Hans Joachim Mette, Karl Schlechta, and Carl Koch, 2nd edn., 5 vols. (Munich: Beck, 1994)

BGE   *Beyond Good and Evil* (1886), trans. Marion Faber (Oxford and New York: Oxford University Press, 1998)

BT   *The Birth of Tragedy* (1872), trans. Douglas Smith (Oxford and New York: Oxford University Press, 2000)

D   *Daybreak* (1881), trans. R. J. Hollingdale (Cambridge: Cambridge University Press, 1982)

GM   *On the Genealogy of Morals* (1887), trans. Douglas Smith (Oxford and New York: Oxford University Press, 1996)

GS   *The Gay Science* (1882–7), trans. Walter Kaufmann (New York: Vintage, 1974)

HA   *Human, All Too Human* (1878–80), trans. R. J. Hollingdale (Cambridge: Cambridge University Press, 1986)

KSA   *Friedrich Nietzsche: Sämtliche Werke. Kritische Studienausgabe*,
        2nd edn., ed. Giorgio Colli and Mazzino Montinari, 15 vols.
        (Munich: dtv; Berlin and New York: de Gruyter, 1988)

KSB   *Friedrich Nietzsche: Sämtliche Briefe. Kritische Studienausgabe*,
        ed. Giorgio Colli and Mazzino Montinari, 8 vols. (Berlin
        and New York: de Gruyter; Munich: dtv, 1986)

TI   *Twilight of the Idols*, trans. Duncan Large (Oxford and New
        York: Oxford University Press, 1998)

UM   *Untimely Meditations* (1873–6), trans. R. J. Hollingdale
        (Cambridge: Cambridge University Press, 1983)

WC   *The Wagner Case* (1888), in *The Birth of Tragedy and
        The Case of Wagner*, trans. Walter Kaufmann (New York:
        Vintage, 1967)

WP   *The Will to Power*, trans. Walter Kaufmann and R. J.
        Hollingdale (New York: Vintage, 1968)

Z   *Thus Spoke Zarathustra* (1883–5), trans. Graham Parkes
        (Oxford and New York: Oxford University Press, 2005)

INTRODUCTION

'And so I tell myself my life'

Nietzsche wrote *Ecce Homo* at the very end of his intellectual career, in the late autumn of 1888, just a few weeks before his catastrophic collapse into insanity at the beginning of January 1889. It was his last original work,[1] and the last of his philosophical works to be published when it eventually appeared in 1908, under the general editorship of his sister. It is customary to describe *Ecce Homo* as 'Nietzsche's autobiography'—indeed this was the spurious subtitle used for the first English translation[2]—and it is a typical autobiography in that it presents the reader with what its author considers to be the most salient features of his life so far, explaining their significance, but it is an atypical autobiography in most other respects. If, as a reader, you come to the book in the expectation of finding anything like a balanced, comprehensive, and objective account of the philosopher's life, usable for reference purposes, then you will be sorely disappointed. It gives readers a few milestone dates from which to take their bearings, but these are relatively few and unevenly dispersed: there are major chronological gaps in the narrative, and a great deal of basic information which one might legitimately expect to be provided in a biographical account is missing. To take one noteworthy example, Nietzsche never even tells us directly when he was born, and instead leaves it to us to reconstruct the date (15 October 1844) from partial information.

---

[1] The two texts on which he worked even after *Ecce Homo* had been started, *Nietzsche contra Wagner* and the *Dithyrambs of Dionysus*, were lightly revised compilations of earlier material.

[2] *Ecce Homo (Nietzsche's Autobiography)*, trans. Anthony M. Ludovici, in Oscar Levy (ed.), *The Complete Works of Friedrich Nietzsche*, 18 vols. (Edinburgh, London, and New York: Foulis, 1909–11), vol. 17 (1911). In all there have been six previous English versions of the complete text, by Ludovici (reprinted Mineola, NY: Dover, 2004), Clifton P. Fadiman (New York: The Modern Library, 1927), Walter Kaufmann (New York: Vintage, 1967), R. J. Hollingdale (Harmondsworth and New York: Penguin, 1979; 2nd edn. 1992), Thomas Wayne (New York: Algora, 2004), and Judith Norman (Cambridge and New York: Cambridge University Press, 2005).

We are able to fill in such gaps, thankfully, because the facts of
Nietzsche's life are by now very well established—through his
own accounts elsewhere, such as in his correspondence, through
first-hand accounts by those who knew him, and through the
accounts of later biographers, by whom he has been very well
served.[3] These allow us to determine that *Ecce Homo* not only
lacks the sort of documentary scaffolding one expects from a biographical account, but that it is positively misleading and inaccur-
ate in many places (it is partial in both senses of the word). So we
can only conclude that Nietzsche does not consider factual historical details to be at all important aspects of his life, that he is not
going to play the autobiographical game in the way we have come
to expect, and prefers instead to subvert the genre. In the spring of
1888 he had been asked by an important early admirer, the Danish
scholar and critic Georg Brandes, for a basic factual account of his
life to underpin the lecture series Brandes was giving on Nietzsche's
philosophy at the University of Copenhagen. This request met with
a positive response—Nietzsche was delighted at such a rare expression of interest in his philosophy—and the result was a 'curricu-
lum vitae' he sent Brandes in a letter of 10 April 1888.[4] Even there
he embellishes the facts and exaggerates a good deal for rhetorical
effect, though—claiming, for example, to have been born 'on the
battlefield of Lützen' when in fact he was born close by, in the
Saxon village of Röcken. Objectivity was never Nietzsche's strong
suit, never even a value he recognized as worth pursuing (witness
the critique of scientific objectivity in the Third Essay of *On the*

---

[3] In the first instance, the reader of this volume is of course referred to the outline
'Chronology of Friedrich Nietzsche', below. The standard biography in German, by
Curt Paul Janz, runs to almost 2,000 pages in three volumes (*Friedrich Nietzsche:
Biographie* (Munich and Vienna: Hanser, 1978–9)); it is complemented by an exhaust-
ive, 800-page chronology of his life: *Friedrich Nietzsche: Chronik in Bildern und Texten*,
ed. Raymond J. Benders and Stephan Oettermann (Munich and Vienna: Hanser, 2000).
The best biographical accounts available in English are listed in the 'Select
Bibliography', below; Sander Gilman's (rather misleadingly titled) *Conversations with
Nietzsche: A Life in the Words of His Contemporaries*, trans. David J. Parent (New York
and Oxford: Oxford University Press, 1987) is a useful collection of portraits by
Nietzsche's friends and relations.
[4] KSB 8: 288–90, reproduced in Keith Ansell Pearson and Duncan Large (eds.), *The
Nietzsche Reader* (Malden, Mass., and Oxford: Blackwell, 2005), 517–19.

Genealogy of Morals), so it is not as though he is just being absent-minded in *Ecce Homo* and would have benefited from being nudged into providing more information by an editor, had the book gone to press in his mentally active lifetime. Instead, the text's whimsicality is a deliberate strategy. If it is not intended as a factual account, though, what is *Ecce Homo*, and what prompted Nietzsche to write it? He does give us a number of positive indications as to what the book is and how he wishes us to read it. Let us consider, first, the circumstances of its composition.

Even for a relatively short book, *Ecce Homo* was completed very quickly: the majority of the text was written over a period of just three weeks, between 15 October and 4 November 1888 (while Nietzsche was also correcting proofs and continuing his various correspondences). Such rapid productivity was in fact quite typical of this *annus mirabilis*, for whereas on average Nietzsche had produced one new book per year since the start of his academic career,[5] *Ecce Homo* was already the fourth he had produced in 1888, preceded by *The Wagner Case*, *Twilight of the Idols*, and *The Antichrist*. The latter two were indeed still pending when he began *Ecce Homo* on his forty-fourth birthday as a birthday present to himself, a thank-offering to his life for the 'succulent fruits' of the recent months and a celebration of the restoration of his health after an extended bout of illness. Nietzsche's interest in autobiography, and biography in general, was very long-standing. His juvenilia include a number of autobiographical sketches describing his childhood and youth;[6] he was always very interested in reading others' journals, memoirs, and correspondence (such as those by the abbé Galiani,[7] the Brothers Goncourt, Charles Baudelaire, and George Sand), and he had included many autobiographical passages in his own mature writings. He had

---

[5] A total of sixteen books in sixteen years—not counting the reprints of the mid-1880s, occasional pieces, his musical composition *Hymn to Life*, etc. For an exhaustive listing of all Nietzsche's works, see William H. Schaberg, *The Nietzsche Canon: A Publication History and Bibliography* (Chicago and London: University of Chicago Press, 1995).

[6] As an example, see 'My Life' (1863), in Ansell Pearson and Large, *Nietzsche Reader*, 18–20.

[7] A draft version of the title page of *Ecce Homo* uses a quotation from Galiani's correspondence as an epigraph (KSA 14: 470).

never attempted anything on this scale before, though, which is why he explains at the beginning of the Foreword what has prompted him to turn to writing *Ecce Homo* precisely at this juncture: 'In view of the fact that I will shortly have to confront humanity with the heaviest demand ever made of it, it seems to me essential to say *who I am*' (F 1).

The most important context for the composition of *Ecce Homo*, then, is not the work he had already completed, but rather a work that was yet to come. The opening reference is to the project on which he had been working in the background since the time of *Thus Spoke Zarathustra* in 1884, amassing a great many preparatory notes towards what he generally referred to as *The Will to Power*, intended as his *magnum opus*. Over the course of 1888 his plans for this work changed markedly—it was retitled and reconceived as *Revaluation of All Values* (*Umwerthung aller Werthe*) before being definitively abandoned shortly before Nietzsche's mental collapse.[8] While he was working on *Ecce Homo*, though, he still had it very much in prospect, and it is important to bear this in mind, since although *Ecce Homo* would turn out to be Nietzsche's final original work, it is quite the opposite of a valediction and has instead the character of an annunciation: like *Beyond Good and Evil* before it, it deserves the subtitle 'Prelude to a Philosophy of the Future'. Nietzsche wrote *Ecce Homo*, and the works of 1888 in general, buoyed by a fond fantasy, in high-spirited anticipation of the momentous impact he was shortly to have on the world by publishing a great summation of his philosophical ideas. As he implies in the dedication, though, he is Janus-faced and also looks back on the past, all too aware of what *little* impact his works have had thus far, how much of a task it has been for him to find public recognition. The point of writing *Ecce Homo* is ostensibly to win himself new readers who will understand him aright, but for the moment his only reliable readership is himself, 'And so I tell myself my life'.

---

[8] See Mazzino Montinari, 'Nietzsche's Unpublished Writings from 1885 to 1888; or, Textual Criticism and the Will to Power', in *Reading Nietzsche*, trans. Greg Whitlock (Urbana and Chicago: University of Illinois Press, 2003), 80–102.

'How To Become What You Are': Education and Exemplarity

Ecce Homo effectively begins by announcing, modestly (and this will be the book's only modesty), 'There cometh one mightier than I after me': it is given the ancillary role of serving the book which is to come, and conceived as a kind of stock-taking exercise. Its task is not to break new philosophical ground, but—like the works which immediately preceded it, *Twilight of the Idols* and *The Antichrist*—to survey the ground already covered over the course of Nietzsche's career thus far. He frequently claims that in order to understand his works a reader needs to have shared his experiences (III 1), so to aid the reader of the *Revaluation* he aims to narrate the formative experiences which made him what he is (the author of the *Revaluation*). *Ecce Homo* is in this sense a work of self-explanation and self-justification, which is why its four chapters are all headed 'Why I . . .': its main aim is to ensure that the author of the *Revaluation* is not misunderstood (F 1).

The book also has its own agenda, though, and fulfils an educative function which is signalled by its subtitle: 'How To Become What You Are' ('Wie man wird, was man ist'). Like *Twilight of the Idols; or, How to Philosophize with a Hammer*, the subtitle to *Ecce Homo* conjures up a kind of instruction manual—but this is an instruction manual like no other, since it reflects Nietzsche's paradigm of how instruction ought to be given. His understanding of the educational relationship is a very specific one which stands in marked contrast to the Gradgrindian norms of his day, with their emphasis on rote learning of factual knowledge.[9] As far as Nietzsche is concerned it is pointless trying to educate by presenting a blueprint for someone else to follow, since human individuality—defined as the particular configuration of each person's drives—dictates that what is optimal for me cannot be optimal for you, in fact is more or less guaranteed not even to be good for you. Just as he poured scorn in *Twilight* (TI VI 1–2) on Luigi Cornaro's best-selling *Discourses on a Life of Temperance* for

---

[9] For his critique of this kind of education (especially what passes for German education), see I 7; II 1; II 3; and III 'UM' 1; see also the chapter of *Twilight of the Idols* on 'What the Germans Lack' (TI VIII).

its effrontery in passing off a specific dietary regime as good for everyone's health, so here he himself refrains from presenting his own life as a recipe to be followed slavishly in every detail. As he puts it in the Foreword: 'The last thing *I* would promise would be to "improve" humanity. I do not set up any new idols' (F 2)—including himself as idol. He does occasionally stoop to giving explicit advice, especially in Chapter 2, but his aim here is much more that of describing himself and his tastes in more general terms so as to serve as a model.

Nietzsche's standard view of the educator, indeed, is that he should be a model ('Vorbild') who stands out ahead of his pupils and, to use the memorable line from the end of Goethe's *Faust II* which Nietzsche never tires of parodying, 'draws us onward and upward' ('zieht uns hinan').[10] This conception of education can be traced back to some of his earliest work—the 1872 lectures 'On the Future of our Educational Institutions',[11] and especially the 1874 *Untimely Meditation* on *Schopenhauer as Educator*, which Nietzsche now admits was actually just a self-portrait (III 'UM' 3). In its Nietzschean inflection, education consists in showing rather than telling; it involves inducing, *educing* the pupil into a self-overcoming, standing above so that those below can learn how to reach one's heights, learn that there are such heights to reach.[12] The greatest instantiation of this doctrine in Nietzsche's philosophy, Nietzsche's greatest teacher figure, is of course his fictional creation Zarathustra,[13] and he closes the Foreword to *Ecce Homo* by quoting extensively from the end of the First Part of his earlier

[10] The analogy is ironic to the extent that the Goethe quotation applies to 'the eternal feminine', while Nietzsche's educators are exclusively masculine.

[11] These have recently become available in a new English translation by Michael W. Grenke (South Bend, Ind.: St Augustine's Press, 2004).

[12] On Nietzsche and education, see: David E. Cooper, *Authenticity and Learning: Nietzsche's Educational Philosophy* (London and Boston: Routledge & Kegan Paul, 1983); Jacques Derrida, 'Otobiographies: The Teaching of Nietzsche and the Politics of the Proper Name', trans. Avital Ronell, in Derrida, *The Ear of the Other: Otobiography, Transference, Translation*, ed. Christie McDonald (New York: Schocken Books, 1985), 1–38; and Michael Peters, James Marshall, and Paul Smeyers (eds.), *Nietzsche's Legacy for Education: Past and Present Values* (Westport, Conn.: Bergin & Garvey, 2001).

[13] See Laurence Lampert, *Nietzsche's Teaching: An Interpretation of 'Thus Spoke Zarathustra'* (New Haven and London: Yale University Press, 1986).

work (using Zarathustra as his proxy, as so often in this text), where Zarathustra takes his leave of his disciples and exhorts them not to blindly follow him (as disciples, 'believers'), but to go their own way: 'Now I bid you lose me and find yourselves' (F 4).

For *Ecce Homo* to be an educational book, then, it needs to pull off the awkward feat of presenting Nietzsche as an aid to *self*-help, *self*-education in others, the goal being to help others achieve ('become') a self in the first place. Rather than urging its readers to 'be themselves'—the mantra of self-help gurus since time immemorial—*Ecce Homo* instead promotes the process of self-becoming as an ethical ideal. What does it mean to become oneself? That is what Nietzsche seeks to demonstrate here, by presenting himself as an inspirational example of successfully achieved selfhood. Although the book is not subtitled 'How I Became What I Am', this is effectively what it explains, and in accordance with Nietzsche's particularizing educational theory (which is antithetical to any kind of universal) this is all it can explain. By these means he will demonstrate what it means to become *a* self, at all. For a self (on this understanding) is not something you just are—you have to achieve it, and keep achieving it over and over again. The ethic of self-becoming in Nietzsche is intimately connected to the strenuous ethic of self-overcoming, that is, overcoming the parts of yourself that are not, ultimately, of yourself or do not, as Nietzsche puts it, belong to your task, your destiny. You must not turn your back on such extraneous, alien elements, though—you must have no regrets, must not disown any part of yourself ('I would not want to abandon an action *after the event*': II 1); rather, you must aim for absolutely inclusive self-ownership. The dynamic of self-overcoming ultimately involves a kind of incorporation, then: you incorporate what was alien into your task by affirming it and deeming it retrospectively to have been a necessary stage in your personal development ('redeeming' it—the only kind of redemption Zarathustra considers worthy of the name (III 'Z' 8)). This is what constitutes Nietzsche's key concept of *amor fati*, or 'love of fate', his 'formula for human greatness': 'not wanting anything to be different, not forwards, not backwards, not for all eternity. Not just enduring what is necessary, still less concealing it [. . .] but *loving* it' (II 10).[14]

As an example of what it means in practice to view one's past in this way we can take Nietzsche's attitude towards his academic career, for although he recognizes it now as a 'mistake', an 'instinctual aberration [. . .] deviating from the *task* of my life' (II 2), nevertheless he can also concede that his time in academia was a *necessary* detour: 'I *had* to be a scholar, too, for a while' (III 'UM' 3). Similarly, although he makes it abundantly clear in *The Wagner Case*, earlier in the year, how much he now despises Wagner, in *Ecce Homo* he can still call Wagner 'the greatest benefactor of my life' (II 6), because in looking back over their relationship he can acknowledge the extent to which Wagner helped him to come to a realization of his own potential. As Zarathustra puts it, the redemption of the past that is *amor fati* means 'to re-create all "It was" into a "Thus I willed it!"' (III 'Z' 8): it requires an artist and involves the creative recrafting of the past to suit the narrative of today, but this retrospective reinterpretation, the retroactive assertion of the will inevitably also involves bending the historical truth to some extent. In the case of Nietzsche's relationship to Wagner, he plays up for effect the 'miraculously meaningful coincidence' which led to Wagner's copy of *Human, All Too Human* crossing in the post with the libretto of *Parsifal* (III 'HA' 5), or the similarly remarkable coincidence that he should have completed Part One of *Thus Spoke Zarathustra* in February 1883 'at precisely the sacred hour when Richard Wagner died in Venice' (III 'Z' 1). More straightforward biographical accounts reveal that in both these cases Nietzsche's version is at variance with the historical truth, and the same can be said for many of the other claims he puts forward here—that he has no personal experience of religious difficulties, for example (II 1), that he never felt better than when writing *Daybreak* (III 'D' 1), or that he has not had a book in his hand for the last six months (II 3), and so on. *Ecce Homo*

---

[14] The evidently paradoxical task of 'becoming what you (already) are' lends itself to interpretation in existentialist terms: the 'natural state' of man is 'bad faith'; the purpose of your life should be to engineer the coincidence of your existence with your essence (fate) by leading your life as a voyage of self-discovery, towards authentic self-realization.

abounds in such gross exaggerations and barefaced lies—what we would nowadays call 'spin-doctoring'—which bring home to the reader the fact that what is being described here is what psychoanalysis would later call a projection, an 'ego ideal'. 'Some day I wish to be only a Yes-sayer', Nietzsche remarked in *The Gay Science* when he first introduced the term '*amor fati*' as his personal goal (GS 276), and *Ecce Homo* is the (fantasmatic) realization of that goal, intended as a testament to Nietzsche's ability to affirm everything about himself in this way, by hook or by crook.

'*The Magic of the Extreme*'

Nietzsche presents the text, then, as an object lesson, and argues that he himself is in all ways best qualified to write this exemplary autobiography, for not only is he the exemplary self-achiever (self-becomer), but he has become an exemplary self which is capable of being absolutely affirmed. In order to appreciate what he has become, moreover, Nietzsche points out that he has had to become the most insightful psychologist there has ever been (III 5)—and Sigmund Freud, for one, lent the claim credence, agreeing that Nietzsche had achieved a 'degree of introspection [that] had never been achieved by anyone'[15]—while the exorbitant claims he makes for his art of style as a writer in Chapter 3 (III 4) ensure that in this respect, too, he has achieved exemplary status. All in all, Nietzsche presents himself here as an exemplary human being (and one of the senses of the phrase '*ecce homo*', indeed, is simply 'behold man'); more than that, he presents himself as 'the type that has turned out best', which he defines with the word 'overman' (III 1).[16]

In *Ecce Homo* Nietzsche makes a series of extraordinarily hyperbolic claims for the self that he has apparently become, its

---

[15] Freud's words to the Vienna Psychoanalytic Society in October 1908 after a reading of *Ecce Homo*. See Herman Nunberg and Ernst Federn (eds.), *Minutes of the Vienna Psychoanalytic Society*, trans. Margarete Nunberg, 4 vols. (New York: International Universities Press, 1962–75), 2: 31–2.

[16] I have used this translation for *Übermensch* throughout, although 'Superman' and 'Overhuman' are also possible.

virtues and achievements, and this is doubtless the first aspect of
the book to strike the reader who just sees the chapter titles on the
contents page. The most conspicuous characteristic of the text is
its boastfulness, its immense immodesty, its euphoric, self-adulatory
tone, and we are simply not used to such heights of self-affirmation
from an author, such a display of monumental egoism.[17] Nietzsche
makes plain his love of hyperbole in a note from the autumn of 1887:
'The spell that fights on our behalf, the eye of Venus that charms
and blinds even our opponents, is the *magic of the extreme*, the
seduction that everything extreme exercises: we immoralists—we
are *the most extreme* . . .' (WP 749/KSA 12: 510). In *Ecce Homo* he
certainly shows himself to have been seduced, but this creates a
real problem for his readers, who may find it rather easier to resist
the lure of Venus' divine charms. *Ecce Homo* undoubtedly polar-
izes the reactions of its readers, for there are various possible
responses to this onslaught of hyperbolic claims. If we are not
willing to grant Nietzsche the benefit of the doubt and concede
that he does write good books, that he is clever, and so on, then
we will doubtless find this book off-putting and object to its grat-
ing tone. In any case we will inevitably want to know whether
Nietzsche is being serious about all this, or whether he is not,
rather, playing a game with us. Is this perhaps not so much an
exemplary autobiography as a spoof, a parody? Might there not,
after all, be an ironic, self-deprecating sense of humour at work (or
play) here, as there is when, a decade later, that most Nietzschean of
composers Richard Strauss, tongue firmly in cheek, casts himself
as the subject of the tone poem 'A Hero's Life' (*Ein Heldenleben*)?
At various points in the course of the text Nietzsche does, after
all, invite us not to take him seriously: 'I know of no other way of
dealing with great tasks than by *playing*' (II 10), he remarks, or
again: 'I don't want to be a saint, and would rather be a buffoon
. . . Perhaps I am a buffoon' (IV 1). In *On the Genealogy of Morals*
Nietzsche mused whether Wagner's *Parsifal* might not have been
intended as the satyr play to round off the composer's tragic

---

[17] Notwithstanding the forty-six instances of the word 'perhaps' (*vielleicht*) in the
text, which Nietzsche frequently uses to qualify his statements.

career (GM III 3), and the same could be said of *Ecce Homo*. After all, Nietzsche also concedes: 'I would prefer to be a satyr rather than a saint' (F 2).

Given the momentousness of the task that he claims to lie ahead of him, though, we must assume that *Ecce Homo*, too, is intended seriously—in the Nietzschean fashion, at least, with its (relentless) cheerfulness and good humour. Another way of contextualizing the book's outrageous claims is to assimilate it into the tradition of self-justifying, self-aggrandizing autobiographies by other nineteenth-century figures who understood themselves, in Romantic fashion, to be geniuses,[18] whether Stendhal's *The Life of Henry Brulard* (1835), Berlioz's *Memoirs* (1870), or most pertinently of all Wagner's *My Life* (1880), which Nietzsche knew intimately since he had supervised its proofing and printing in 1869/70.[19] In this context, in this company, it is a moot point whether Nietzsche's self-advertising text is actually all that outlandish after all—at any rate it is clear that it is not *sui generis*, he is not redefining the genre, but rather just taking the generic immodesty of the autobiography to its extreme (the difference is a question of degree rather than of kind).

A further point to bear in mind in seeking to understand Nietzsche's hyperbolic approach is what one might call the ontological status of the self for whom such extraordinary capacities and achievements are being claimed. Before we become outraged at the book and provoked beyond measure by its impostures, we need to bring to bear a literary-critical awareness of the work as a crafted fiction, as a kind of *Bildungsroman*, indeed, with its leading protagonist, 'Nietzsche', as effectively a literary construct, a fictional character, like the thinly veiled self-representation that is Stendhal's 'Henry Brulard'. As we have seen, *Ecce Homo* is not so much self-serving as self-creating, and the Nietzsche who emerges from this work (the ego ideal) bears as much relation to the historical figure as does, for example, Zarathustra to the historical Zoroaster.

---

[18] Cf. IV 1: '*Revaluation of all values*: that is my formula for the highest act of self-reflection on the part of humanity, which has become flesh and genius in me.'

[19] See Schaberg, *Nietzsche Canon*, 15.

As he himself says at the beginning of Chapter 3, 'I am one thing, my writings are another' (III 1), and this apotropaic statement needs to be taken self-reflexively to refer to the 'I' who is the product of this writing, too. Alexander Nehamas points out: 'Nietzsche himself . . . is a creature of his own texts'; he makes an 'effort to create an artwork out of himself, a literary character who is a philosopher',[20] and nowhere is this effort more in evidence than in *Ecce Homo*, although in this respect, once again, the book merely brings to a culmination what is a feature of Nietzsche's other, earlier works, too, where 'giving style to one's character' (GS 290), or 'fashioning oneself into a whole', as in the presentation of Goethe in *Twilight* (TI IX 49), is presented as the highest desideratum, the 'one thing needful'.

A final explanation for the hyperbolic excesses of the book has been to accuse its author of having already passed beyond the edge of reason and to see it as a document of insanity—a testament not so much to the heights of self-knowledge as to the depths of self-delusion. With hindsight, for example, one can readily interpret the overly affirmative tone of the book as indicative of the state of euphoria which often precedes the onset of tertiary syphilis, but it would be going too far to dismiss the book on that account. Undeniably some of Nietzsche's late interpolations—for example, the controversial paragraph which he substituted as the third section in Chapter 1, and which talks in apparently megalomaniacal fashion of his 'divinity'[21]—show signs of incipient insanity, but such passages do not necessarily disqualify the work as philosophy. When Nietzsche's 'dynamite' does explode at the beginning of January 1889, he identifies himself with 'every name in history' (KSB 8: 578) and begins signing his letters with multiple signatures; in *Ecce Homo*, though, a centripetal force is still at work as Nietzsche 'harvests' all the multiple identities he has been obliged to adopt so far (Schopenhauer and Wagner, Zarathustra, Paul Rée, etc.), fashioning them into a single (albeit fictionalized)

---

[20] Alexander Nehamas, *Nietzsche: Life as Literature* (Cambridge, Mass., and London: Harvard University Press, 1985), 8.

[21] For full details, see Mazzino Montinari, 'A New Section in Nietzsche's *Ecce Homo*', in *Reading Nietzsche*, 103–40.

self which is 'schizophrenic' only to the extent that it has to split itself in order to narrate (itself to itself) at all.[22]

Ecce Homo *as Philosophy: Major Themes*

Just as *Ecce Homo* takes an existing literary genre (the Romantic autobiography of the genius-hero) and pushes it to the limit, so too it merely takes to rhetorical extremes the assertion of Nietzsche's earlier philosophical positions. As we have seen, he promises no radical departures in the text—this is not the work with which he plans to rock the world to its foundations—and as a result it is, philosophically speaking, relatively low-key. The philosophical arguments put forward here are perfectly coherent in their own right and can coexist with his earlier works. The major late themes—*amor fati*, eternal recurrence, the overman, will to power— are all in evidence here to some extent, but they are not made the focus of the argument. Similarly, what new themes are introduced—'Russian fatalism' (I 6) or the '*rancune* of the great' (III 'Z' 5)—are limited in their scope.

Nevertheless, in addition to its being an exemplary autobiography, Nietzsche aims for *Ecce Homo* to be an exemplary work of philosophy, and the co-incidence of the two is no coincidence, for he is presenting (this kind of) autobiography *as* exemplary philosophy. Philosophy to Nietzsche means living a certain kind of life: the two are inextricably intertwined, so that life writing also makes for the best philosophy. In *Beyond Good and Evil* he

---

[22] On the motif of the harvest, see not only the dedication (the paragraph intercalated between the Foreword and the main text) but also Nietzsche's letter of 18 October to his friend Overbeck: 'I am now the most grateful man in the world—autumnally minded in every good sense of the word; it is my great *harvest time*' (*Selected Letters of Friedrich Nietzsche*, ed. and trans. Christopher Middleton (Chicago and London: University of Chicago Press, 1969; repr. Indianapolis: Hackett, 1996), 315). On the fissures in Nietzsche's autobiographical subject, see: Sarah Kofman, 'Explosion I: Of Nietzsche's *Ecce Homo*', trans. Duncan Large, *Diacritics*, 24/4 (1994), 51–70, repr. in Daniel W. Conway with Peter S. Groff (eds.), *Nietzsche: Critical Assessments*, 4 vols. (London and New York: Routledge, 1998), 1: 218–41; and Daniel W. Conway, 'Nietzsche's *Doppelgänger*: Affirmation and Resentment in *Ecce Homo*', in Keith Ansell-Pearson and Howard Caygill (eds.), *The Fate of the New Nietzsche* (Aldershot and Brookfield, Vt.: Avebury, 1993), 55–78.

remarks: 'Little by little I came to understand what every great philosophy to date has been: the personal confession of its author, a kind of unintended and unwitting memoir' (BGE 6). *Ecce Homo* represents the inversion of this perspective, then: Nietzsche's confessional philosophy will be a conscious memoir and will not seek to hide its biographical roots as all previous great philosophies have, ashamed of them, but, rather, will parade them.[23] As he puts it early on in the first chapter: 'I turned my will to health, to *life*, into my philosophy' (I 2). We have seen that the existential theme of self-achievement provides an overarching meta-structure to the book as a whole; in its other main themes, *Ecce Homo* acts as a continuation of Nietzsche's four previous works and the critiques they contain. Specifically, it continues the critique of morality from *On the Genealogy of Morals*, the critique of Wagner, the Germans, and (German) political nationalism from *The Wagner Case*, the critique of idealism from *Twilight of the Idols*, and the critique of Christianity from *The Antichrist*. Such an enumeration might suggest that the book is another of Nietzsche's 'no-saying' writings, but—as he himself stresses—*Ecce Homo* is an affirmative work and to each of these critiques he offers an affirmative alternative.

From its blasphemous title (which Nietzsche was the first to use for a self-referential work)[24] to its antagonistic final stand-off between pagan and Christian deities, via Nietzsche's repeated self-descriptions as 'wicked', 'the Antichrist' (III 2), and so on, the tone of anti-Christian condemnation runs right through *Ecce Homo* like a red thread. The text's anti-Christianity is above all an attack on what Nietzsche views as the most pernicious form of idealism to have devalued life thus far (II 2), and to emphasize his contempt for this kind of other-worldliness he resolves to adopt

---

[23] Here Nietzsche's project in *Ecce Homo* is entirely misunderstood by Martin Heidegger in his attempt to rescue Nietzsche from accusations of 'biologism'. See Heidegger, *Nietzsche*, ed. David Farrell Krell, trans. David Farrell Krell *et al.*, 4 vols. (San Francisco and London: Harper & Row, 1979–87), 3: 39–47.

[24] Many previous works had been given the title, but these were devotional publications of one kind or another, such as Sir John Robert Seeley's popular *Ecce homo: A Survey of the Life and Works of Jesus Christ* (London: MacMillan, 1866). One of Nietzsche's aims in publishing his book with this title was to test the Prussian censorship laws—see his letter to Köselitz of 30 October 1888 (Middleton, *Selected Letters*, 319).

the perspective of 'life' against Christianity (IV 7), remaining firmly earth-bound, immanent, and materialist. In his notebooks of this late period Nietzsche constantly reminds himself to philosophize 'using the body as a guide',[25] and *Ecce Homo* is a striking instantiation of such a body-philosophy. Zarathustra had condemned Christians as 'despisers of the body'; here, Nietzsche presents instead his 'bodily wisdom' through his preference for the workings of the digestive tract over the 'mind' or 'spirit' (*Geist*) and a privileging of the earthiest of the senses, the sense of smell, over the others ('My genius is in my nostrils': IV 1).[26] His anti-idealism, moreover, takes on methodological proportions, too, in the form of what we might call (after Jean-François Lyotard) an aversion to 'grand narrative',[27] what he had called in the *Genealogy* (GM III 24) a '*petit faitalisme*', a fatalism of little facts, with which the text positively bristles, resulting in a curious juxtaposition of the banal and the heroic—or rather in the banal presented *as* heroic. Who would have thought that in preparation for the imminent *Revaluation* Nietzsche-as-overman should deem it necessary to correct a printer's error in the score of his *Hymn to Life* (III 'Z' 1)?

In a text so determinedly devoted to a presentation of techniques for becoming a self, it is hardly surprising if the aspect of Christianity to which Nietzsche objects most vehemently is its 'morality of unselfing oneself' (III 'D' 2; IV 7), which he condemns as the morality of 'decadence' par excellence (IV 7). In this light the text's monumental immodesty and egoism appear as anti-Christian strategies, but more important is the positive, affirmative strategy that Nietzsche also adopts, namely his assertion of 'immoralism'. No fewer than four times in the text does Nietzsche claim to be 'the first *immoralist*' (III 'UM' 2; III 'HA' 6; IV 2; IV 3), and he also

---

[25] See KSA 11: 249, 282, 565 (WP 659), 578, 623, 692; KSA 12: 92, 106 (WP 518).

[26] For the thematization of smells and smelling, see also: I 1; I 8; III 'BT' 1–2; III 'D' 1; and III 'Z' 4. On the bodily in general, see esp. Rodolphe Gasché, '*Ecce Homo* or the Written Body', trans. Judith Still, *Oxford Literary Review*, 7/1–2 (1985), 3–24; repr. in *Looking After Nietzsche*, ed. Laurence A. Rickels (Albany, NY: SUNY Press, 1990), 113–36.

[27] See Lyotard, *The Postmodern Condition: A Report on Knowledge*, trans. Geoff Bennington and Brian Massumi (Minneapolis: University of Minnesota Press; Manchester: Manchester University Press, 1984).

(rightly) lays claim to having coined the term in the first place (IV 4). As in *The Antichrist* (AC 61), here, too, Nietzsche lays the blame for the persistence of Christianity into the present age firmly at the door of the Protestant Reformation led by Martin Luther (III 'WC' 2); nor is that the only calamity for which he holds the German nation responsible, since Wagner was irredeemably and unforgivably corrupted when he 'went among Germans' (as among swine).[28] Once again, though, Nietzsche is at pains to turn his critique into an affirmation: in this case the obverse of his Germanophobia is his Francophilia, above all—the only literature for which he professes an interest is French (II 3), and he deems Paris to be the artist's only home in Europe (II 5). Of the ninety-nine people named in *Ecce Homo*, over a quarter are French, or honorary French (Chopin and Cosima Wagner)—it is the second most common nationality after the forty-two Germans, and far ahead of the eight Italians in third place.[29] Typically of Nietzsche's 1888 texts in general, too, French-derived loan-words and quotations are liberally scattered across the text. Equally, though, he holds up Venice as a synonym for musicality (II 7), and in his own case he asserts a family legend (since disproved) concerning the Nietzsches' Polish origins.[30]

The presentation of his own genealogy (in the orthodox sense) provides the riddling opening of the first chapter of the book.[31] In this chapter as a whole Nietzsche establishes general principles

[28] Cf. Letter to Brandes, 20 Nov. 1888: 'Can you guess who comes off worst in *Ecce Homo*? The Germans!' (Middleton, *Selected Letters*, 326).

[29] The full tallies are: 42 German, 26 French, 8 Italian, 6 British, 5 Greek, 3 Roman, 2 Russian and Swiss, 1 Danish, Hungarian, Nepalese, Norwegian, and Persian.

[30] See Sarah Kofman, 'A Fantastical Genealogy: Nietzsche's Family Romance', trans. Deborah Jenson, in *Nietzsche and the Feminine*, ed. Peter J. Burgard (Charlottesville: University Press of Virginia, 1994), 35–52.

[31] On the opening riddle and its interpretations, see: Tracy B. Strong, 'Oedipus as Hero: Family and Family Metaphors in Nietzsche', in Daniel T. O'Hara (ed.), *Why Nietzsche Now?* (Bloomington and London: Indiana University Press, 1985), 311–35; David Farrell Krell, 'Consultations with the Paternal Shadow: Gasché, Derrida, and Klossowski on *Ecce Homo*', in Krell and David Wood (eds.), *Exceedingly Nietzsche: Aspects of Contemporary Nietzsche-Interpretation* (London and New York: Routledge, 1988), 80–94; and Jean Graybeal, '*Ecce Homo*: Abjection and "the Feminine"', in Kelly Oliver and Marilyn Pearsall (eds.), *Feminist Interpretations of Friedrich Nietzsche* (University Park: Pennsylvania State University Press, 1998), 152–69.

about his descent and his decadence, and affirms the overcoming of decadence in his own case; he displays the marks of his ascent which constitute the 'wisdom' of his ethics, the character or self that he has become, together with its 'aristocratic' values. By contrast, the 'cleverness' (or 'craftiness': *Klugheit*) to which he lays claim in the second chapter is more mundane, and consists rather in a series of tastes and techniques which he has arrived at by means of his psycho-physiological self-analysis, culminating in the declaration of (self-)love that is the expression of the principle of *amor fati*. The third chapter is mainly devoted to passing under review Nietzsche's earlier works, but in the first five paragraphs he discusses their reception and the style of their writing. He freely admits that his earlier work has generally been misunderstood but, undaunted, turns this into a badge of honour and argues that his 'good books' have simply not yet found the right readers—'some are born posthumously' (III 1). The presentations of his earlier writings in the third chapter (and elsewhere in the book, too, as in his copious self-laudatory comments on *Zarathustra*) are actually no different from the presentation of his life, for here, too, *Ecce Homo* plays fast and loose with historical detail, extracting from his earlier texts (most notably the earliest of them, *The Birth of Tragedy*) only what he now deems worthy of surviving. This principle of self-reinterpretation had already been applied in the additional prefaces Nietzsche wrote for the second editions of many of his works in the period 1885–6; once again, though, *Ecce Homo* brings this trend to a culmination. In the fourth and final chapter the tone turns positively apocalyptic, with Nietzsche claiming to be 'the man of impending disaster' (IV 1) and 'by far the most terrifying human being there has ever been' (IV 2). Consistent with the strenuous ethic of self-overcoming, then, the final chapter shows him straining to escape the very bounds of humanity, asserting his 'divinity' once again at the last, through an identification with the tragic god Dionysus.

Given the exorbitant, hyperbolic qualities of *Ecce Homo*, it is hardly surprising that the book has proved decidedly uncomfortable reading over the years and been accorded a 'Cinderella' status among

Nietzsche's works, suffering a prolonged and systematic marginalization. Nietzsche himself was unable to complete the text before his descent into madness, and his sister Elisabeth then withheld it from publication for twenty years till 1908, when it finally appeared in a prohibitively expensive 'bank director's edition', after which it struggled to be accorded a place in the Nietzsche canon until the Colli–Montinari edition of 1969 finally established a conclusive version of the text. The critical reception of *Ecce Homo* has mirrored this marginalization in a surprisingly faithful way, too, and despite, for example, Oscar Levy's deeming it one of the six volumes of the English *Complete Works* which 'may be strongly recommended as containing the quintessence of Nietzsche',[32] as recently as 1988 Robert C. Solomon and Kathleen M. Higgins still omit *Ecce Homo* from their canon of prescribed texts for students *Reading Nietzsche*.[33] *Ecce Homo*, it seems, is still proving awkward in some quarters, though this is by now atypical: thankfully it has seen something of a renaissance in popularity over recent years, and a monumental two-part commentary published in 1992–3 by the French philosopher Sarah Kofman (to whose memory this translation is dedicated) emphatically confirmed the rehabilitation of Nietzsche's most ill-treated text.[34] 'If I conjure up the image of a perfect reader,' Nietzsche writes (III 3), 'it always turns into a monster of courage and curiosity, and what's more something supple, cunning, cautious, a born adventurer and discoverer.' There is doubtless something monstrous about *Ecce Homo*, but there is equally no doubt that—on the eve of the centenary of its first publication—it still deserves to be read: as a beautifully written book, as one of the most sparkling, witty works of life-literature that we possess, and as the summation of an extraordinary philosophical career, a last great testament to Nietzsche's will.

[32] Part of his advice to readers reproduced at the back of each volume of his edition.

[33] Robert C. Solomon and Kathleen M. Higgins (eds.), *Reading Nietzsche* (New York and Oxford: Oxford University Press, 1988). For further details on the reception history, see Duncan Large, 'Double "Whaam"! Sarah Kofman on *Ecce Homo*', *German Life and Letters*, 48/4 (1995), 441–62.

[34] See Sarah Kofman, *Explosion I: De l''Ecce Homo' de Nietzsche* (Paris: Galilée, 1992), and *Explosion II: Les Enfants de Nietzsche* (Paris: Galilée, 1993).

NOTE ON THE TEXT AND TRANSLATION

The text on which this translation is based is the standard German edition, *Ecce homo. Wie man wird, was man ist*, prepared by Giorgio Colli and Mazzino Montinari (KSA 6: 255–374). Where possible I have retained Nietzsche's idiosyncratic punctuation, which the Colli–Montinari edition restores after previous editors discreetly standardized it. Instances of Nietzsche's double emphasis have been rendered in bold type. I am grateful to my colleague Fritz Gregor Herrmann, with whom I discussed parts of the final draft of the translation, and to Graham Parkes for permission to reprint substantial excerpts from his Oxford World's Classics translation of *Thus Spoke Zarathustra*.

In preparing the explanatory notes and glossary of names I have benefited from consulting the notes and index to the Colli–Montinari *Kritische Studienausgabe* and to other editions of the text by Peter Pütz and Eric Blondel. In addition to glossing Nietzsche's references and allusions I have tried to alert the reader to any linguistic play which could not be adequately conveyed by the translation itself, to provide as many cross-references within the text as might be useful, and to relate its arguments and stylistic features to those of Nietzsche's other works.

In preparing the introduction I have drawn on some material previously published in Duncan Large, 'Double "Whaam"! Sarah Kofman on *Ecce Homo*', *German Life and Letters*, 48/4 (1995), 441–62, and Keith Ansell Pearson and Duncan Large (eds.), *The Nietzsche Reader* (Malden, Mass., and Oxford: Blackwell, 2005), 439–50. I am grateful to Ritchie Robertson for giving me the opportunity to present a first version of the introduction as a paper in the seminar series 'Teaching Nietzsche' at Oxford University.

Finally I should like to thank my editor Judith Luna for her expert advice and abiding support.

SELECT BIBLIOGRAPHY

The following is a list of selected secondary works on Nietzsche in English. In addition, two academic journals are exclusively devoted to publishing articles on Nietzsche in English: the *Journal of Nietzsche Studies*, published by the Pennsylvania State University Press on behalf of the Friedrich Nietzsche Society (UK), and *New Nietzsche Studies*, published by the Nietzsche Society (USA). Each year the Fall issue of *International Studies in Philosophy* (Binghamton University, NY) contains a selection of papers delivered to the North American Nietzsche Society, and the yearbook *Nietzsche-Studien* (Berlin and New York: de Gruyter) contains articles in English as well as German, French, and Italian.

Biographies of Nietzsche

Bergmann, Peter, *Nietzsche: 'The Last Antipolitical German'* (Bloomington and Indianapolis: Indiana University Press, 1987).

Cate, Curtis, *Friedrich Nietzsche* (London: Hutchinson, 2002).

Chamberlain, Lesley, *Nietzsche in Turin: The End of the Future* (London: Quartet, 1996); repr. as *Nietzsche in Turin: An Intimate Biography* (New York: Picador, 1998).

Gilman, Sander L. (ed.), *Conversations with Nietzsche: A Life in the Words of His Contemporaries*, trans. David J. Parent (New York and Oxford: Oxford University Press, 1987).

Hayman, Ronald, *Nietzsche: A Critical Life* (London: Weidenfeld & Nicolson; New York: Oxford University Press, 1980).

Hollingdale, R. J., *Nietzsche: The Man and his Philosophy*, 2nd edn. (Cambridge and New York: Cambridge University Press, 1999).

Krell, David Farrell, and Donald L. Bates, *The Good European: Nietzsche's Work Sites in Word and Image* (Chicago and London: University of Chicago Press, 1997).

Safranski, Rüdiger, *Nietzsche: A Philosophical Biography*, trans. Shelley Frisch (New York: Norton; London: Granta, 2002).

Verrecchia, Anacleto, *La catastrofe di Nietzsche a Torino* (Turin: Einaudi, 1978).

Introductions to Nietzsche's Work

Ansell Pearson, Keith, *An Introduction to Nietzsche as Political Thinker: The Perfect Nihilist* (Cambridge: Cambridge University Press, 1994).

—— *How to Read Nietzsche* (London: Granta Books, 2005).

—— and Duncan Large (eds.), *The Nietzsche Reader* (Malden, Mass., and Oxford: Blackwell, 2005).

Danto, Arthur C., *Nietzsche as Philosopher*, 2nd edn. (New York: Columbia University Press, 2005).

Fink, Eugen, *Nietzsche's Philosophy*, trans. Goetz Richter (London and New York: Continuum, 2003).

Kaufmann, Walter, *Nietzsche: Philosopher, Psychologist, Anti-Christ*, 4th edn. (Princeton, NJ, and London: Princeton University Press, 1974).

Solomon, Robert C., and Kathleen M. Higgins (eds.), *Reading Nietzsche* (New York and Oxford: Oxford University Press, 1988).

Stern, J. P., *A Study of Nietzsche* (Cambridge and New York: Cambridge University Press, 1979).

Vattimo, Gianni, *Nietzsche: An Introduction*, trans. Nicholas Martin (London: Continuum; Stanford, Calif.: Stanford University Press, 2002).

Major Critical Studies and Collections

Allison, David B. (ed.), *The New Nietzsche: Contemporary Styles of Interpretation*, 2nd edn. (Cambridge, Mass., and London: MIT Press, 1985).

Ansell Pearson, Keith (ed.), *A Companion to Nietzsche* (Malden, Mass., and Oxford: Blackwell, 2006).

Clark, Maudemarie, *Nietzsche on Truth and Philosophy* (Cambridge and New York: Cambridge University Press, 1990).

Conway, Daniel W., *Nietzsche and the Political* (London and New York: Routledge, 1997).

—— with Peter S. Groff (eds.), *Nietzsche: Critical Assessments*, 4 vols. (London and New York: Routledge, 1998).

Deleuze, Gilles, *Nietzsche and Philosophy*, trans. Hugh Tomlinson (London: Athlone Press; New York: Columbia University Press, 1983).

Derrida, Jacques, *Spurs: Nietzsche's Styles/Éperons: Les Styles de Nietzsche*, trans. Barbara Harlow (Chicago and London: University of Chicago Press, 1979).

Heidegger, Martin, *Nietzsche*, ed. David Farrell Krell, trans. David Farrell Krell *et al.*, 4 vols. (San Francisco and London: Harper & Row, 1979–87).

Kofman, Sarah, *Nietzsche and Metaphor*, trans. Duncan Large (London: Athlone Press; Stanford, Calif.: Stanford University Press, 1993).

Leiter, Brian, *Nietzsche on Morality* (London and New York: Routledge, 2002).

Magnus, Bernd, and Kathleen M. Higgins (eds.), *The Cambridge Companion to Nietzsche* (Cambridge and New York: Cambridge University Press, 1996).

Müller-Lauter, Wolfgang, *Nietzsche: His Philosophy of Contradictions and the Contradictions of his Philosophy*, trans. David J. Parent (Urbana and Chicago: University of Illinois Press, 1999).

Nehamas, Alexander, *Nietzsche: Life as Literature* (Cambridge, Mass., and London: Harvard University Press, 1985).

Oliver, Kelly, and Marilyn Pearsall (eds.), *Feminist Interpretations of Friedrich Nietzsche* (University Park: Pennsylvania State University Press, 1998).

Parkes, Graham, *Composing the Soul: Reaches of Nietzsche's Psychology* (Chicago and London: University of Chicago Press, 1994).

Pasley, Malcolm (ed.), *Nietzsche: Imagery and Thought. A Collection of Essays* (London: Methuen; Berkeley and Los Angeles: University of California Press, 1978).

Richardson, John, and Brian Leiter (eds.), *Nietzsche* (Oxford and New York: Oxford University Press, 2001).

Schacht, Richard, *Nietzsche* (London and Boston: Routledge & Kegan Paul, 1983).

Sedgwick, Peter R. (ed.), *Nietzsche: A Critical Reader* (Oxford and Cambridge, Mass: Blackwell, 1995).

Strong, Tracy B., *Friedrich Nietzsche and the Politics of Transfiguration*, 3rd edn. (Urbana and Chicago: University of Illinois Press, 2000).

Further Reading on Ecce Homo

Badiou, Alain, 'Who is Nietzsche?', trans. Alberto Toscano, *Pli*, 11 (2001), 1–12.

boundary 2, 9/3 and 10/1 (Spring/Fall 1981): 'Why Nietzsche Now? A *boundary 2* Symposium', subsequently republished as Daniel T. O'Hara (ed.), *Why Nietzsche Now?* (Bloomington and London: Indiana University Press, 1985). Includes essays on *Ecce Homo* by Charles Altieri ('Ecce Homo: Narcissism, Power, Pathos, and the Status of Autobiographical Representations', 389–413), Rodolphe Gasché ('Autobiography as *Gestalt*: Nietzsche's *Ecce Homo*', 271–90), and Hugh J. Silverman ('The Autobiographical Textuality of Nietzsche's *Ecce Homo*', 141–51), in addition to a review of Hollingdale's 1979 translation by Taffy Martin ('Selecting, Arranging, Interpreting: Reading Nietzsche Reading Nietzsche', 417–24). Tracy B. Strong's

'Oedipus as Hero: Family and Family Metaphors in Nietzsche' (pp. 311–35) also addresses the text.

Conway, Daniel W., 'Nietzsche's *Doppelgänger*: Affirmation and Resentment in *Ecce Homo*', in Keith Ansell-Pearson and Howard Caygill (eds.), *The Fate of the New Nietzsche* (Aldershot and Brookfield, Vt.: Avebury, 1993), 55–78.

Derrida, Jacques, 'Otobiographies: The Teaching of Nietzsche and the Politics of the Proper Name', trans. Avital Ronell, in Derrida, *The Ear of the Other: Otobiography, Transference, Translation*, ed. Christie McDonald (New York: Schocken Books, 1985), 1–38.

Gasché, Rodolphe, '*Ecce Homo* or the Written Body', trans. Judith Still, *Oxford Literary Review*, 7/1–2 (1985), 3–24; repr. in *Looking After Nietzsche*, ed. Laurence A. Rickels (Albany, NY: SUNY Press, 1990), 113–36.

Graybeal, Jean, '*Ecce Homo*: Abjection and "the Feminine"', in Oliver and Pearsall, *Feminist Interpretations*, 152–69.

Kofman, Sarah, *Explosion I: De l' 'Ecce Homo' de Nietzsche* (Paris: Galilée, 1992). Two excerpts have been published in English so far: 'Explosion I: Of Nietzsche's *Ecce Homo*', trans. Duncan Large, *Diacritics*, 24/4 (1994), 51–70; repr. in Conway with Groff, *Critical Assessments*, 1: 218–41) and 'A Fantastical Genealogy: Nietzsche's Family Romance', trans. Deborah Jenson, in *Nietzsche and the Feminine*, ed. Peter J. Burgard (Charlottesville: University Press of Virginia, 1994), 35–52.

—— *Explosion II: Les Enfants de Nietzsche* (Paris: Galilée, 1993). Two excerpts have been published in English so far: 'Accessories (*Ecce Homo*, "Why I Write Such Good Books", "The Untimelies", 3)', trans. Duncan Large, in Sedgwick, *Critical Reader*, 144-57, and 'The Psychologist of the Eternal Feminine', trans. Madeleine Dobie, *Yale French Studies*, 87 (1995), 173–89.

Krell, David Farrell, 'Consultations with the Paternal Shadow: Gasché, Derrida, and Klossowski on *Ecce Homo*', in Krell and David Wood (eds.), *Exceedingly Nietzsche: Aspects of Contemporary Nietzsche-Interpretation* (London and New York: Routledge, 1988), 80–94.

Large, Duncan, 'Double "Whaam"! Sarah Kofman on *Ecce Homo*', *German Life and Letters*, 48/4 (1995), 441–62.

Montinari, Mazzino, 'A New Section in Nietzsche's *Ecce Homo*', in Montinari, *Reading Nietzsche*, trans. Greg Whitlock (Urbana and Chicago: University of Illinois Press, 2003), 103–40.

Parker, David, 'Nietzsche's Ethics and Literary Studies: A Reading of *Ecce Homo*', *Cambridge Quarterly*, 33/4 (2004), 299–314.

Platt, Michael, 'Behold Nietzsche', *Nietzsche-Studien*, 22 (1993), 42–79.

Pletsch, Carl, 'The Self-Sufficient Text in Nietzsche and Kierkegaard', *Yale French Studies*, 66 (1984), 160–88.

Samuel, Richard, 'Friedrich Nietzsche's *Ecce Homo*: An Autobiography?', in *Deutung und Bedeutung: Studies in German and Comparative Literature Presented to Karl-Werner Maurer*, ed. Brigitte Schludermann *et al.* (The Hague: Mouton, 1973), 210–27.

Shapiro, Gary, 'How One Becomes What One Is Not (*Ecce Homo*)', in *Nietzschean Narratives* (Bloomington and Indianapolis: Indiana University Press, 1989), 142–67.

Steinbuch, Thomas, *A Commentary on Nietzsche's 'Ecce Homo'* (Lanham, Md., and London: University Press of America, 1994).

Further Reading in Oxford World's Classics

Nietzsche, Friedrich, *Beyond Good and Evil*, trans. Marion Faber, introduction by Robert C. Holub.

—— *The Birth of Tragedy*, trans. Douglas Smith.

—— *On the Genealogy of Morals*, trans. Douglas Smith.

—— *Thus Spoke Zarathustra*, trans. Graham Parkes.

—— *Twilight of the Idols*, trans. Duncan Large.

A CHRONOLOGY OF
FRIEDRICH NIETZSCHE

1844   Friedrich Wilhelm Nietzsche born in Röcken (Saxony) on 15 October, son of Carl Ludwig and Franziska Nietzsche. His father and both grandfathers are Protestant clergymen.

1846   Birth of sister Elisabeth.

1849   Birth of brother Joseph; death of father.

1850   Death of brother; family moves to Naumburg.

1858–64 Attends renowned boys' boarding-school Pforta, where he excels in classics. Begins to suffer from migraine attacks which will plague him for the rest of his career.

1864   Enters Bonn University to study theology and classical philology.

1865   Follows classics professor Ritschl to Leipzig University, where he drops theology and continues with studies in classical philology. Discovers Schopenhauer's philosophy and becomes a passionate admirer.

1867   Begins publishing career with essay on the Greek lyric poet Theognis; continues publishing philological articles and book reviews till 1873.

1867–8 Military service in Naumburg, until invalided out after a riding accident.

1868   Back in Leipzig, meets Richard Wagner for the first time and quickly becomes a devotee. Increasing disaffection with philology: plans to escape to Paris to study chemistry.

1869   On Ritschl's recommendation, appointed Extraordinary Professor of Classical Philology at Basle University. Awarded doctorate without examination; renounces Prussian citizenship. Begins a series of idyllic visits to the Wagners at Tribschen, on Lake Lucerne. Develops admiration for Jacob Burckhardt, his new colleague in Basle.

1870   Promoted to full professor. Participates in Franco-Prussian War as volunteer medical orderly, but contracts dysentery and diphtheria at the front within a fortnight.

1871   Granted semester's sick-leave from Basle and works intensively on *The Birth of Tragedy*. Germany unified; founding of the Reich.

1872 Publishes *The Birth of Tragedy out of the Spirit of Music*, which earns him the condemnation of professional colleagues. Lectures 'On the Future of our Educational Institutions'; attends laying of foundation stone for Bayreuth Festival Theatre.

1873 Publishes first *Untimely Meditation: David Strauss, the Confessor and the Writer*.

1874 Publishes second and third *Untimely Meditations: On the Uses and Disadvantages of History for Life* and *Schopenhauer as Educator*. Relationship with Wagner begins to sour.

1875 Meets musician Heinrich Köselitz (Peter Gast), who idolizes him.

1876 Publishes fourth and last *Untimely Meditation: Richard Wagner in Bayreuth*. Attends first Bayreuth Festival but leaves early and subsequently breaks with Wagner. Further illness; granted full year's sick-leave from the university.

1877 French translation of *Richard Wagner in Bayreuth* published, the only translation to appear during his mentally active lifetime.

1878 Publishes *Human, All Too Human: A Book for Free Spirits*, which confirms the break with Wagner.

1879 Publishes supplement to *Human, All Too Human, Assorted Opinions and Maxims*. Finally retires from teaching on a pension; first visits the Engadine, summering in St Moritz.

1880 Publishes final supplement to *Human, All Too Human, The Wanderer and His Shadow*. First stays in Venice and Genoa.

1881 Publishes *Daybreak: Thoughts on the Prejudices of Morality*. First stay in Sils-Maria.

1882 Publishes *The Gay Science*. Infatuation with Lou von Salomé, who spurns his marriage proposals.

1883 Publishes *Thus Spoke Zarathustra: A Book for Everyone and Nobody*, Parts I and II (separately). Death of Wagner. Spends the summer in Sils and the winter in Nice, his pattern for the next five years. Increasingly consumed by writing.

1884 Publishes *Thus Spoke Zarathustra*, Part III.

1885 *Thus Spoke Zarathustra*, Part IV printed but circulated to only a handful of friends. Begins in earnest to amass notes for *The Will to Power*.

1886 Publishes *Beyond Good and Evil: Prelude to a Philosophy of the Future*. Change of publisher results in new expanded editions of *The Birth of Tragedy* and *Human, All Too Human* (now with a second volume comprising the *Assorted Opinions and Maxims* and *The Wanderer and His Shadow*).

1887 Publishes *On the Genealogy of Morals: A Polemic*. New, expanded editions of *Daybreak* and *The Gay Science*.

1888 Begins to receive public recognition: Georg Brandes lectures on his work in Copenhagen. Discovers Turin, where he writes *The Wagner Case: A Musician's Problem*. Abandons *The Will to Power*, then completes in quick succession: *Twilight of the Idols; or, How to Philosophize with a Hammer* (first published 1889), *The Antichrist: Curse on Christianity* (first published 1895), *Ecce Homo: How To Become What You Are* (first published 1908), *Nietzsche contra Wagner: Documents of a Psychologist* (first published 1895), and *Dithyrambs of Dionysus* (first published 1892).

1889 Suffers mental breakdown in Turin (3 January) and is eventually committed to asylum in Jena.

1890 Discharged into the care of his mother in Naumburg.

1894 Elisabeth founds Nietzsche Archive in Naumburg (moving it to Weimar two years later).

1897 Mother dies; Elisabeth moves her brother to Weimar.

1900 Friedrich Nietzsche dies in Weimar on 25 August.

ECCE HOMO

How To Become What You Are

FOREWORD

1

In view of the fact that I will shortly have to confront humanity with the heaviest demand ever made of it, it seems to me essential to say *who I am*. People ought really to know already: for I have not failed to 'bear witness' to myself.* But the mismatch between the greatness of my task and the *smallness* of my contemporaries has been evident in the fact that I have not been heard or even just seen. I am living on my own credit; perhaps it is merely a prejudice that I am alive at all?... I need only talk with one or other of the 'educated people' who come to the Upper Engadine* in the summer to convince myself that I am *not* alive... Under these circumstances there is a duty against which my habit, and even more so the pride of my instincts, fundamentally rebels, namely to say: *listen to me! for I am such and such. Above all, don't mistake me!*

2

I am, for instance, definitely no bogeyman, no moral monster— I am by nature even the opposite of the type of person who has been admired as virtuous till now. Between ourselves, it seems to me that that is precisely something I can be proud of. I am a disciple of the philosopher Dionysus;* I would prefer to be a satyr rather than a saint. But just read this work. Perhaps I have managed to express this contrast in a cheerful and benevolent way, perhaps that was the only point of this work. The last thing *I* would promise would be to 'improve' humanity. I do not set up any new idols; let the old ones learn what it means to have legs of clay. *Toppling idols* (my word for 'ideals')—that is more my kind of handiwork. Reality has been robbed of its value, its sense, its truthfulness insofar as an ideal world was *faked up*... The 'real world' and the 'apparent world'— in plain words: the *fake* world and reality*... The *lie* of the ideal has till now been the curse on reality; on its account humanity itself has become fake and false right down to its deepest instincts—to the point of worshipping values *opposite* to the only ones which would guarantee it a flourishing, a future, the exalted *right* to a future.

3

—Anyone who knows how to breathe the air of my writings knows that it is an air of the heights, a *bracing* air. You must be made for it, or else you are in no little danger of catching cold in it. The ice is near, the solitude is immense—but how peacefully everything lies in the light! how freely you breathe! how much you feel to be *beneath* you!—Philosophy, as I have understood and lived it so far, is choosing to live in ice and high mountains—seeking out everything alien and questionable in existence, everything that has hitherto been excluded by morality. From the long experience which such a wandering *in the forbidden* gave me, I learnt to view the reasons people have moralized and idealized so far very differently from what may be wished: the *hidden* history of philosophers, the psychology of their great names came to light for me.—How much truth can a spirit* *stand*, how much truth does it *dare*?—for me that became more and more the real measure of value. Error (belief in the ideal) is not blindness, error is *cowardice*... Every achievement, every step forwards in knowledge is the *consequence* of courage, of toughness towards oneself, of sincerity* towards oneself... I do not refute ideals, I just put gloves on to protect myself against them... *Nitimur in vetitum:** under this sign my philosophy will triumph one day, for the only thing that has been altogether forbidden so far is the truth.—

4

—Among my writings my *Zarathustra* stands alone. With it I have given humanity the greatest gift it has ever been given. This book, with a voice that stretches over millennia, is not only the most exalted book there is, the real book of the mountain air—the entire fact of man lies at a vast distance *beneath* it—it is also the *most profound* book, born of the innermost richness of the truth, an inexhaustible well into which no bucket descends that does not come back up filled with gold and goodness. Here speaks no 'prophet', none of those gruesome hybrids of sickness and will to power* called founders of religions. Above all you have to *hear* properly the tone that comes out of this mouth, this halcyon tone, if you are not to be pitifully unjust towards the meaning of its wisdom. 'It is the stillest words that bring on the storm; thoughts that come on doves' feet direct the world—'*

> The figs are falling from the trees, they are good and sweet: and as they fall, their red skins burst. A north wind am I to all ripe figs.
> And thus, like figs, these teachings fall to you, my friends: now drink their juice and their sweet flesh! Autumn is all around and clear sky and afternoon—*

These are not the words of a fanatic, this is not 'preaching', no *faith* is being demanded here: drop after drop, word upon word falls from an infinite abundance of light and depth of happiness—the tempo of these speeches is a delicate slowness. The like of this reaches only the most select; it is a peerless privilege to be a listener here; no one is at liberty to have ears for Zarathustra... Is Zarathustra with all that not a *seducer*?... But what does he himself say when he returns to his solitude for the first time? Precisely the opposite of what some 'sage', 'saint', 'world-redeemer', or other *décadent** would say in such a situation... He not only speaks differently, he *is* just different...

> Alone I go now, my disciples! You too must go away now, and alone!* Thus I will it.
> Go away from me and guard yourselves against Zarathustra! And better still: be ashamed of him! Perhaps he has deceived you.
> The man of understanding must be able not only to love his enemies, but also to hate his friends.
> One repays a teacher poorly if one always remains only a student. And why would you not pluck at my wreath?
> You revere me: but what if your reverence should some day *collapse*? Be careful lest a statue fall and kill you!*
> You say you believe in Zarathustra? But what does Zarathustra matter! You are my believers, but what do any believers matter!
> You had not yet sought yourselves: then you found me. Thus do all believers; that is why all belief is worth so little.
> Now I bid you lose me and find yourselves; and only *when you have all denied me** will I return to you...*

Friedrich Nietzsche

* * *

On this perfect day, when everything is ripening and not only the grapes are turning brown, a shaft of sunlight has just fallen on my life: I looked backwards, I looked ahead, I never saw so much and such good things all at once. Not for nothing have I buried my forty-fourth year today;* I was *entitled* to bury it—all the life that was in it is saved, is immortal. The *Revaluation of All Values*,* the *Dionysus Dithyrambs*, and, by way of recuperation, the *Twilight of the Idols*—all of them gifts of this year, even of its last quarter! *How should I not be grateful to my whole life?* And so I tell myself my life.

* * *

WHY I AM SO WISE

I

The fortunate thing about my existence, perhaps its unique feature, is its fatefulness:* to put it in the form of a riddle, as my father I have already died, as my mother I am still alive and growing old. This twofold provenance, as it were from the top and bottom rungs on the ladder of life, both *décadent* and *beginning*—this, if anything, explains the neutrality, the freedom from bias in relation to the overall problem of life, that perhaps distinguishes me. I have a finer nose for the signs of ascent and descent than any man has ever had; I am the teacher par excellence in such matters—I know both, I am both.—My father died at the age of 36:* he was delicate, kindly, and morbid, like a being destined only to pass by—more a gracious remembrance of life than life itself. In the same year as his life declined, mine declined, too: in the thirty-sixth year of my life I reached the nadir of my vitality—I was still alive, but could not see three steps ahead of me. At that point—it was 1879— I resigned my professorship in Basle, lived through the summer like a shadow in St Moritz and the following winter, the least sunny of my life, *as* a shadow in Naumburg.* This was my minimum: *The Wanderer and his Shadow* was produced while it was going on. Without a doubt I was an expert in shadows in those days... The following winter, my first in Genoa, the sweetening and spiritual-ization that are more or less bound to result from extreme anaemia and atrophying of the muscles produced *Daybreak*. The consum-mate brightness and cheerfulness, even exuberance of spirit which this same work reflects can coexist in me not only with the most profound physiological debility, but even with an excessive feeling of pain. Amid the torments brought on by three days of unremitting headache accompanied by the arduous vomiting of phlegm, I pos-sessed a dialectician's clarity par excellence and very cold-bloodedly thought through things for which, in healthier circumstances, I am not enough of a climber, not cunning, not *cold* enough. My readers perhaps know how much I consider dialectics to be a symptom of *décadence*, for example in the most famous case of all, the case of Socrates.*—All sickly disorders of the intellect, even that half-dazed state which follows a fever, have remained to this day totally alien to me, and I had to teach myself about their nature and frequency in an academic manner. My blood runs slowly. No one has ever managed to detect a fever in me. A doctor who treated me for quite a while for a nervous disease ended up saying: 'No! your nerves are not the problem; I'm the one who's nervous.' No sign at all of any kind of local degeneration; no stomach complaint for organic reasons, however much the gastric system is profoundly weakened as a result of general exhaustion. Even the eye complaint, at times verging dangerously on blindness, just a consequence, not causal: so that with every increase in vitality the eyesight has picked up again, too.—A long, all-too-long succession of years mean in my case convalescence—unfortunately they also mean lapsing, relapsing, periodically a kind of *décadence*. Do I need say, after all that, that in questions of *décadence* I am *experienced*? I have spelt it out forwards and backwards. Even that filigree art of grasping and comprehending in general, those fingers for nuances, that psychology of 'seeing round the corner', and whatever else is characteristic of me, was learnt only then and is the true gift of that time when everything in me was being refined, observation itself as well as all the organs of observation. Looking from the perspective of the sick towards *healthier* concepts and values, and conversely looking down from the fullness and self-assuredness of *rich* life into the secret workings of the *décadence* instinct—this is what I practised longest, this was my true experience; if I became master of anything then it was of this. I have my hand in now, I am handy* at *inverting perspectives*: the foremost reason why for me alone perhaps a 'revaluation of values' is even possible.—

2

Aside from being a *décadent*, then, I am also the opposite. My proof of this is, among other things, that I always instinctively chose the *right* means of dealing with unfavourable conditions: while the *décadent* as such always chooses the means that are harmful to him.

As *summa summarum** I was healthy, as nook, as speciality I was *décadent*. That energy to achieve absolute isolation and release from routine circumstances, the pressure on myself forcing me not to let myself be taken care of, waited on, *doctored with* any longer—they betray an absolute instinctual certainty about *what*, above all, was required at that stage. I took myself in hand, I made myself healthy again: the prerequisite for this—as every physiologist will concede—is *that one is basically healthy*. A typically morbid being cannot become healthy, still less make itself healthy; for a typical healthy person, conversely, being ill can even be an energetic *stimulant* to living, to living more. This, indeed, is how that long period of illness appears to me *now*: it was as if I discovered life anew, myself included; I tasted all the good things, even the small ones, as no other could easily taste them—I turned my will to health, to *life*, into my philosophy... For take note: the years when my vitality was at its lowest were when I *stopped* being a pessimist:* the instinct for self-recovery *forbade* me a philosophy of poverty and discouragement... And basically how do you tell if someone has *turned out well!** By the fact that someone who has turned out well is good for our senses: the stuff he is made of is at once hard, delicate, and fragrant. Only what he finds conducive is to his taste; his pleasure, his enjoyment stops when the mark of what is conducive is overstepped. He guesses correctly what will heal harm, he exploits strokes of bad luck to his advantage; what does not kill him makes him stronger.* Instinctively he gathers together from everything he sees, hears, experiences, *his* aggregate: he is a selective principle, he lets a great deal go. He is always in *his* kind of company, whether he is dealing with books, people, or landscapes: he honours by *choosing*, by *granting admission*, by *trusting*. He reacts to every kind of stimulus slowly, with the slowness which years of caution and a willed pride have cultivated in him—he examines the stimulus as it approaches and has no intention of going to meet it. He does not believe in either 'misfortune' or 'guilt': he copes, with himself and with others, he knows how to *forget*—he is strong enough for everything to *have* to turn out for the best with him.—Well then, I am the *opposite* of a *décadent*: for I have just been describing *myself*.

3

I consider it a great privilege to have had such a father: the farmers to whom he preached—for after he had lived several years at the Altenburg court,* in his last years he was a preacher—said that that was how an angel must look.—And with this I touch on the question of pedigree. I am a Polish nobleman *pur sang*,* with which not a drop of bad blood is mixed, least of all German blood. When I look for my profoundest opposite, ineradicable vulgarity of the instincts, I always find my mother and sister—to think of myself as related to such *canaille** would be a blasphemy against my divinity. The treatment I have experienced at the hands of my mother and sister, right up to this moment, fills me with unspeakable horror: here a perfectly infernal machine is at work, unerringly sure of the moment when a bloody wound can be inflicted on me— in my most exalted moments... for at such times one lacks all power to defend oneself against poisonous vermin... Physiological contiguity makes such a *disharmonia praestabilita** possible... But I confess that the most profound objection against the 'eternal recurrence',* my truly *abyssal* thought, is always mother and sister. —But even as a Pole I am a tremendous atavism. You would have to go back centuries to find this race, the noblest there has ever been on earth, quite so instinctually pure as I represent it. I have a sovereign feeling of distinction compared to everything that is nowadays called *noblesse*—I would not grant the young German Kaiser* the honour of being my coachman. There is but one instance where I acknowledge an equal—I confess it with profound gratitude. Frau Cosima Wagner is by far the noblest of natures; and so as not to say a word too little, I say that Richard Wagner was the man who was by far the most closely related to me... The rest is silence*... All the prevailing notions about degrees of relatedness are the most outrageous kind of physiological nonsense. The Pope* is even today trading on such nonsense. You are *least* related to your parents: it would be the most extreme sign of vulgarity to be related to one's parents. The higher natures have their origin infinitely further back; they have had to be collected, saved, accumulated for, for the longest time.* The *great* individuals

are the oldest: I do not understand it, but Julius Caesar could
be my father—*or* Alexander, that Dionysus incarnate... At this
moment, as I am writing this, the postman brings me a Dionysus
head...*

4

I have never understood the art of taking against me—I have my
incomparable father to thank for that, too—and even when it
seemed of great value to me. I have never even taken against
myself—however unchristian that may seem. Examine my life
from any angle you like, and you will find no trace (excepting that
one instance)* of anyone having had any ill will towards me—but
perhaps rather too many traces of *good* will... My experiences
even with those of whom everyone else has bad experiences speak
without exception in their favour; I tame every bear, I make even
the buffoons mind their manners. In the seven years when I taught
Greek to the top class of the grammar school in Basle,* I never
had occasion to impose a punishment; the laziest worked hard
for me. I am always a match for a chance occurrence; I need to be
unprepared to be master of myself. Whatever the instrument—
even if it is as out of tune as only the instrument 'man' can go out
of tune—I would have to be ill not to succeed in getting something listenable-to out of it. And how often have I heard from
the 'instruments' themselves that they have never heard themselves sounding like *that*... The finest example of this was perhaps Heinrich von Stein, who died unforgivably young: once,
after carefully obtaining permission, he turned up in Sils-Maria*
for three days, explaining to everyone that he had *not* come for the
Engadine. For those three days it was as though this splendid man, who had waded with all the impetuous naivety of a
Prussian junker into the Wagnerian swamp (—and the Dühringian
one, too!), had been transformed by a storm-wind of freedom, like
someone who is suddenly raised up to *his* height and given wings.
I always told him it was the good air up there that was doing it and
everyone was affected in the same way—we were not 6,000 feet
above Bayreuth* for nothing—but he wouldn't believe me...

If nonetheless many a misdeed, large and small, has been perpetrated against me, it was not because of 'the will', least of all any *ill* will: as I just indicated, I should rather have to complain about the good will that has caused me no little trouble in my life. My experiences give me a right to be thoroughly mistrustful of the so-called 'selfless' drives, of all 'brotherly love'* ready with word and deed. In itself it strikes me as a weakness, a specific instance of the inability to resist stimuli—only *décadents* call *compassion* a virtue. I hold it against the compassionate that they easily lose sight of shame, reverence, sensitivity to distances, that in a trice compassion smells of plebs and looks for all the world like bad manners—that compassionate hands may even wreak utter destruction as they plunge into a great destiny, an isolation among wounds, a *right* to a heavy burden of guilt. I count the overcoming of compassion among the *noble* virtues: I wrote about one instance as 'The Temptation of Zarathustra',* when a great cry of distress reaches him and compassion, like one last sin, wants to ambush him and lure him away from *himself*. Keeping control here, keeping the *heights* of his task untainted by the much baser and more short-sighted impulses at work in the so-called selfless actions, this is the test, perhaps the last test, a Zarathustra has to pass—the real *proof* of his strength…

5

In another respect, too, I am just being my father once again and, as it were, his continuing life after an all-too-early death. Like anyone who has never lived among his equals and who has as little purchase on the concept of 'retaliation' as, for instance, on the concept of 'equal rights', in cases where a minor or *very great* act of folly is committed against me I forbid myself any countermeasure, any protective measure—likewise, as is only proper, any defence, any 'justification'. My kind of retaliation consists in sending something clever to chase after stupidity as quickly as possible: that way you may just catch it up. Metaphorically speaking: I send a pot of preserves to get rid of a *sour* story… One need only do something bad to me and I will 'repay' it, of that one can be sure: presently I will find an opportunity to express my thanks to the

'wrongdoer' (occasionally even for the wrongdoing)—or to *ask*
him for something, which can be more obliging than giving something... It seems to me, furthermore, that even the rudest word,
the rudest letter is more good-natured, more honourable than
silence. Those who keep quiet almost always lack refinement and
heartfelt courtesy; silence is an objection, swallowing things necessarily makes for a bad character—it even ruins the stomach.
The silent are all dyspeptic.—You can see that I would not want
rudeness to be underestimated; it is by far the most *humane* form
of contradiction and, in the midst of modern mollycoddling, one
of our foremost virtues.—If you are rich enough to deal with it,
it is even a stroke of luck to be wrong. If a god came to earth, he
should *do* nothing but wrong: assuming not the punishment but
the *guilt*—*that* would be divine.*

6

Freedom from resentment,* enlightenment about resentment—
who knows what great debt of gratitude I ultimately owe my long
illness in this respect, too! The problem is not exactly simple: you
need to have experienced it from a position of strength and from
one of weakness. If anything at all needs to be counted against
being ill, being weak, then it is the fact that in that state the true
healing instinct, in other words the *instinct for defence and weapons*
in man, is worn down. You cannot get rid of anything, you cannot
cope with anything, you cannot fend anything off—everything
hurts you. People and things get intrusively close, experiences
affect you too deeply, memory is a festering wound. Being ill *is* a
kind of resentment itself.—The invalid has only one great remedy
for it—I call it *Russian fatalism*, that fatalism without rebellion
with which a Russian soldier who starts finding the campaign too
hard finally lies down in the snow. Not taking, taking on, taking *in*
anything at all any more—no longer reacting at all... The great
good sense about this fatalism (which is not always just courage
unto death), what makes it life-preserving amidst the most life-
threatening of circumstances, is the reduction of the metabolism,
the slowing of its rate, a kind of will to hibernation. Take this

logic a few steps further and you have the fakir sleeping in a tomb
for weeks on end... Since you would exhaust yourself too quickly
if you reacted at all, you no longer react in any way: such is the
logic. And nothing burns you up faster than the emotions of
resentment. Anger, sickly vulnerability, powerlessness to take
revenge, the lust, the thirst for revenge, every kind of poisonous
troublemaking—for the exhausted this is certainly the most detrimental way of reacting: it brings on a rapid consumption of nervous strength, a sickly intensification of harmful excretions, for
example of bile in the stomach. For the invalid, resentment is the
absolute forbidden—*his* evil: unfortunately his most natural incli-
nation, too.—This is what that profound physiologist Buddha
understood. His 'religion', which ought rather to be called a *hygiene*
so as not to conflate it with such wretched things as Christianity,
made its effect conditional on defeating resentment: liberating the
soul from *that*—first step towards recovery. 'Not through enmity
does enmity come to an end; enmity comes to an end through
friendship':* this stands at the beginning of Buddha's teaching—
this is *not* morality speaking, but physiology.—Resentment, born
of weakness, harms no one more than the weak person himself—
or else, when a rich nature is the premise, it is a *superfluous* feeling,
and to retain mastery over it is practically the proof of richness.
Anyone who knows how seriously my philosophy has taken up
the fight against feelings of revenge and reaction, right down to
the doctrine of 'free will'—the fight against Christianity is just a
specific instance—will understand why I am disclosing at this
point in particular my personal conduct, my *instinctual certainty*
in practice. In times of *décadence* I *forbade* myself them as harmful;
as soon as life was rich and proud enough once again, I forbade
myself them as *beneath* me. That 'Russian fatalism' of which I was
speaking came to the fore in my own case in that for years I doggedly
stuck by almost unbearable situations, places, lodgings, groups of
people, once I had chanced upon them—it was better than
changing them, than *feeling* them to be changeable, than rebelling
against them... If I was disturbed in this fatalism, violently awak-
ened, I was mortally offended in those days—in truth it was indeed
deadly dangerous every time.—Treating oneself as a fate, not

wanting oneself to be 'otherwise'—in such circumstances this is
great good sense itself.

7

Another thing is war.* I am naturally warlike. Attacking is one of
my instincts. Being *able* to be an enemy, being an enemy—these
require a strong nature, perhaps; in any case every strong nature
presupposes them. It needs resistances, so it *seeks* resistance:
aggressive pathos* is just as integrally necessary to strength as the
feeling of revenge and reaction is to weakness. Woman, for
instance, is vengeful:* that is a condition of her weakness, as is her
sensitivity to other people's afflictions.—The strength of an
attacker can in a way be *gauged* by the opposition he requires; all
growth makes itself manifest by searching out a more powerful
opponent—or problem: for a philosopher who is warlike challenges
problems to duels, too. The task is *not* to master all resistances,
but only those against which one has to pit one's entire strength,
suppleness, and mastery-at-arms—opponents who are *equal*...
Equality before the enemy—first precondition for an *honest* duel.
If you despise, you *cannot* wage war; if you command, if you look
down on something, you do not *need* to wage war.—My practice
of war can be summed up in four propositions. First: I attack only
causes that are victorious—on occasion, I wait till they are victorious. Second: I attack causes only when there are no allies to be
found, when I am standing alone—when I am compromising
myself alone... I have never made a move in public that was not
compromising: this is *my* criterion for right action. Third: I never
attack people—I make use of a person only as a kind of strong
magnifying glass with which one can make visible some general
but insidious and quite intangible exigency. This is how I attacked
David Strauss,* or more precisely the *success* of a decrepit book
among the 'educated' in Germany—I caught this education
red-handed... This is how I attacked Wagner,* or more precisely
the falsity, the instinctual indistinction of our 'culture', which mistakes the sophisticated for the rich, the late for the great. Fourth:
I attack things only when all personal disagreement is ruled out,

when there is no background of bad experiences. On the contrary, attacking is for me a proof of benevolence, even of gratitude. By linking my name with that of a cause or a person—whether for or against is indifferent to me—I honour them, I set them apart. When I wage war on Christianity, I am entitled to do so because I have not experienced any fatalities or hindrances from that quarter—the most earnest Christians have always been favourably disposed towards me. I myself, an opponent of Christianity *de rigueur*,* have no intention of holding against an individual what has been the disaster of millennia.—

8

May I make so bold as to intimate one last trait of my nature which causes me no little trouble in my dealings with people? I have an instinct for cleanliness that is utterly uncanny in its sensitivity, which means that I can physiologically detect—*smell*—the proximity or (what am I saying?) the innermost aspect, the 'innards' of every soul... I have psychological feelers attached to this sensitivity, with which I test every secret by touch and get a grip on it: almost on first contact, I am already conscious of the large amount of *concealed* dirt at the bottom of many a nature, perhaps occasioned by bad blood but whitewashed over by upbringing. If my observations were correct, natures like this which are unconducive to my cleanliness feel the circumspection of my disgust on their part, too: it does not make them smell any more pleasant... As has always been my custom—extreme honesty with myself is the prerequisite of my existence; impure conditions are the death of me—I am constantly swimming and bathing and splashing in water, as it were, in some perfectly transparent and sparkling element. This makes dealing with people quite a trial of my patience; my humaneness consists *not* in sympathizing with someone, but in *putting up with* the fact that I sympathize with them... My humaneness is a constant self-overcoming.*—But I need *solitude*, in other words convalescence, a return to myself, the breath of free, light, playful air... The whole of my *Zarathustra* is a dithyramb to solitude, or, if I have been understood,* to *purity*...

Thankfully not to *pure folly*.*—Those who have eyes for colours will call it adamantine.*—*Disgust* at man, at the 'riff-raff', has always been my greatest danger... Do you want to hear the words Zarathustra uses to speak of *deliverance* from disgust?

Yet what happened to me? How did I redeem myself from disgust? Who rejuvenated my eye? How did I fly to heights where no more rabble sits at the well?

Did my disgust itself create wings for me and water-divining powers? Verily, into the highest heights I had to fly, that I might find again the fount of pleasure!—

And find it I did, my brothers! Here in the heights the fount of pleasure wells up for me! And there is a life at which no rabble drinks too!

Almost too violently you stream for me, spring of pleasure! And often you empty the cup again, through wanting so much to fill it.

And still must I learn to approach you more moderately: all too violently does my heart still stream toward you:

—my heart, upon which my summer burns, short, hot, heavy-hearted, over-blissful: how my summer-heart craves your coolness!

Gone the hesitant sorrow of my spring! Passed on the snowflakes of my wickedness in June! Summer have I become entirely, and summer-midday—

—a summer in the highest heights, with cold springs and blissful stillness: oh come, my friends, that the stillness might become even more blissful!

For these are *our* heights and our home: too high and boldly we live here for all unclean creatures and their thirst.

Just cast your clear eyes into the fount of my pleasure, you friends! How could that make it turbid! It shall laugh back to you with *its* own clarity.

In the tree called Future we build our nests; eagles shall bring to us lonely ones victuals in their beaks!

Verily, no victuals that the unclean might share with us! They would think that they were eating fire and would burn their mouths.

Verily, no homes do we hold ready here for the unclean! To their bodies our happiness would be an ice-cave, and to their spirits too!

And like strong winds we would live above them, neighbours to eagles, neighbours to snow, neighbours to the sun: thus do strong winds always live.

And like a wind I would blow them asunder one day and with my spirit take their spirit's breath away: thus my future wills it.

Verily, a strong wind is Zarathustra to all low-lying lands; and this counsel does he give to his enemies and to all that spits and spews: beware of spitting *into* the wind!*...

WHY I AM SO CLEVER

I

—Why do I know a thing or two *more*? Why am I generally so clever? I have never thought about questions that are not real ones—I have not squandered myself.—I have no personal experience, for example, of true *religious* difficulties. I am entirely at a loss to know how 'sinful' I am supposed to be. Likewise I have no reliable criterion for what a pang of conscience is: from what one *hears* about it, a pang of conscience seems to me unworthy of respect... I would not want to abandon an action *after the event*; I would prefer to leave the bad outcome, the *consequences* out of the question of value altogether. If the outcome is bad, it is all too easy to lose the *correct* perspective on what you have done: a pang of conscience seems to me a kind of '*evil* eye'. Cherishing something that goes wrong all the more *because* it went wrong—that is more my kind of morality.—'God', 'immortality of the soul', 'redemption', 'hereafter': all of them concepts to which I have never paid any attention, or given any time, even as a child*—perhaps I was never childish enough for them?—Atheism is not at all familiar to me as a result, still less as an event: it is self-evident to me from instinct. I am too curious, too *dubious*, too high-spirited to content myself with a rough-and-ready answer. God is a rough-and-ready answer, an indelicacy against us thinkers—basically even just a rough-and-ready *prohibition* on us: you shall not think!*... In a quite different way I am interested in a question on which the 'salvation of humanity' depends more than on any curio of the theologians: the question of *nutrition*. For ease of use, one can put it in the following terms: 'how do *you* personally have to nourish yourself in order to attain your maximum of strength, of *virtù* in the Renaissance style,* of moraline-free virtue?'*—In this respect my experiences are as bad as can be; I am amazed at how late I heard this question, how late I learnt from these experiences to see 'reason'. Only the complete worthlessness of our German education*—its 'idealism'—can go some way towards explaining to me why I lagged behind in this of all respects, to the point of holiness. This 'education', which teaches you to lose sight of *realities* from the outset, so as to hare off after utterly problematic, so-called 'ideal' goals, for example 'classical education'—as if combining 'classical' and 'German' in one concept were not doomed from the outset! It is even funny—just think of a 'classically educated' Leipziger!—In actual fact, till my most mature years I only ever ate *badly*—in moral terms, 'impersonally', 'selflessly', 'altruistically', for the good of cooks and other fellow-Christians. Through Leipzig cooking, for example, and at the same time my first study of Schopenhauer (1865), I was very seriously denying my 'will to life'.* How to ruin one's stomach, too, for the sake of insufficient nutrition—said cooking seemed to me to solve this problem with astonishing success. (They say that 1866 was a turning point in this regard—.*) But German cooking in general— what does it not have on its conscience! Soup *before* the meal (called '*alla tedesca*'* even in sixteenth-century Venetian cookbooks), overcooked meat, greasy, mealy vegetables, pastries degenerating into paperweights! If you add on top of all this the positively swinish way older Germans—but by no means just the *older* ones—need to wash everything down, then you can also under-stand where the *German spirit* comes from—from distressed intestines... The German spirit is a case of indigestion—it can never be done with anything.—But the *English* diet, too—which, in comparison with the German, even the French, is a kind of 'return to nature',* in other words to cannibalism—is profoundly at odds with my own instinct; it seems to me that it gives the spirit *heavy* feet—the feet of Englishwomen... The best cooking is the *Piedmontese*.*—Alcoholic drinks are bad for me; a single glass of wine or beer in the course of the day is quite enough to make my life a 'vale of tears'—Munich is where my antipodes live. I may have grasped this rather late, but I have actually been *experiencing* it since childhood. When I was a boy I used to think that drinking wine, like smoking tobacco, was at first just a young man's *vanitas*, then a bad habit. Perhaps the Naumburg wine bears its share of the blame for this *harsh* judgement.* To believe that wine *cheers you up* I would need to be a Christian, in other words believe what to me especially is an absurdity.* Strangely enough, given how extremely easily I am upset by small, heavily diluted doses of alcohol, I practically turn into a sailor when it comes to *strong* doses. Even when I was a boy this was my form of bravery. Writing a long Latin composition, and then even copying it out, in a single all-night sitting, my pen filled with the ambition to imitate the stringency and concision of my model Sallust, and steeping my Latin in some of the highest-strength grog—when I was a pupil at the venerable Schulpforta* this did not contradict my physiology in the slightest, nor even perhaps that of Sallust, for all that it contradicted the venerable Schulpforta... Later on, towards the middle of my life, I of course set my face more and more strictly *against* all 'spirituous' drinks: an opponent of vegetarianism from experience—just like Richard Wagner, who converted me—I cannot recommend strongly enough to all *more spiritual* natures absolute abstinence from alcoholic drinks. *Water* does the job... I prefer places which give you the opportunity everywhere to draw water from running fountains (Nice, Turin, Sils); a little glass follows me around like a dog. *In vino veritas:** it seems even here I disagree with everyone else once again about the concept of 'truth'—in my case the spirit moves over *water**... A few more hints from my morality. A big meal is easier to digest than one that is too small. The first prerequisite of good digestion is that the stomach as a whole should be actively involved. You must *know* the size of your stomach. Inadvisable for the same reason are those long-drawn-out meals which I call sacrificial feasts with intermissions, meals at the table d'hôte.—No snacks, no coffee: coffee makes you gloomy. *Tea* beneficial only in the morning. A little, but strong; tea is very harmful and makes you feel sickly all day if it is just slightly too weak. Everyone has his own level here, often between the tightest and most delicate limits. In a very *agaçant** climate it is inadvisable to begin with tea: one should lead off with a cup of thick, oil-less cocoa an hour beforehand.— *Sit* as little as possible; do not believe any idea that was not born in the open air and of free movement—in which the muscles do not also revel. All prejudices emanate from the bowels.—Sitting still (I said it once already)—the real *sin* against the holy ghost.*—

2

Intimately related to the question of nutrition is the question of *place* and *climate*. No one is at liberty to live everywhere, and anyone who has to perform great tasks that call for all his strength has indeed a very limited choice in this respect. The influence of climate on the *metabolism*—slowing it down, speeding it up—is so extensive that a mistake over place and climate can not only alienate someone from their task but can keep it from them entirely: they never get to see it. They never have enough animal vigour to achieve the freedom that overflows into the most spiritual realm, when someone realizes 'Only I can do *that*'... Once even a little sluggishness of the bowels becomes a bad habit, it is quite enough to turn a genius into something mediocre, something 'German'; the German climate alone is sufficient to discourage strong, even heroically disposed bowels. The tempo of the metabolism stands in precise relation to the agility or lameness of the spirit's *feet*; the 'spirit' itself is, after all, just a mode of this metabolism. Make a list for yourself of the places where intelligent people are and have been, where wit, cunning, malice made people happy, where genius was almost obliged to make its home: all of them have outstandingly dry air. Paris, the Provence, Florence, Jerusalem, Athens—these names prove something: genius *depends* on dry air, on clear skies—in other words on rapid metabolism, on the possibility of supplying oneself with great, even enormous quantities of strength time and again. I can recall a case where, merely for want of instinctual subtlety in matters climatic, an eminent and freely disposed spirit became constricted, crabbed, a specialist and sourpuss. And I myself might ultimately have gone the same way, had illness not forced me to see sense, to reflect on the good sense in reality. Now that, after long years of practice, I read off the effects climate and meteorology have on me as if I were a very finely calibrated and reliable instrument, and on even a short journey, such as from Turin to Milan, register the change in humidity through my own physiology, I am horrified to think of the *uncanny* fact that my life up till ten years ago—the years of deadly danger—always only played itself out in places that were wrong and practically *forbidden* to me. Naumburg, Schulpforta, Thuringia in general, Leipzig, Basle—so many hapless haunts for my physiology. If I have not a single welcome memory of my entire childhood and youth, it would be foolish to ascribe this to so-called 'moral' causes—such as the indisputable lack of *adequate* company: for this lack is there today as it always was, but it does not stop me being cheerful and brave. No, ignorance *in physiologicis**—that confounded 'idealism'—is the real disaster in my life, the superfluous and stupid part of it, something from which nothing good has grown, which cannot be compensated for, cannot be offset. I count as consequences of this 'idealism' all my mistakes, all the great instinctual aberrations and 'modesties' deviating from the *task* of my life, for instance my becoming a philologist—why not a doctor, at least, or something else eye-opening? In my time in Basle my entire spiritual diet, including my daily schedule, was an utterly senseless abuse of extraordinary energies, without a supply of energies in any way covering the consumption, without even any reflection on consumption and replacement. There was a complete lack of the subtler kind of selfishness, of a commanding instinct's *care*; it was treating oneself as equivalent to everyone else, a 'selflessness', a forgetting of one's distance—something I will never forgive myself. When I was almost done for—*because* I was almost done for—I started to reflect on this absurdity fundamental to my life—'idealism'. *Illness* was what made me see reason.—

3

One's choice in nutrition, one's choice of climate and place—the third area in which one must avoid a mistake at all costs is in the choice of *one's kind of relaxation*. Here, too, the limits on what a spirit is allowed, in other words what is *useful* to it, become tighter and tighter the more *sui generis* it is. In my case all *reading* is a relaxation: hence it is one of those things that release me from myself, that let me stroll among alien sciences and souls—that I stop taking seriously. For reading is a release from *my* seriousness. When I am deep in hard work there are no books to be seen around me: I would take care not to let anyone near me speak or even think. And that is what reading is... Has anyone actually noticed that in that state of profound tension to which pregnancy condemns the spirit and basically the whole organism, a chance occurrence, any kind of external stimulation has too violent an effect, 'sinks in' too deep? You have to avoid chance occurrences, external stimuli as much as possible; a kind of self-immurement is one of the foremost instinctual ruses of spiritual pregnancy. Shall I allow an *alien* thought to climb secretly over the wall?— And that is what reading is... After the periods of work and fruitfulness comes the period of relaxation: out you come, you pleasant, intellectually stimulating books I have been shying away from!— Will they be German books?... I have to go back half a year to catch myself with a book in my hand. What was it, though?—An excellent study by Victor Brochard, *Les Sceptiques grecs*, which puts even my Laertiana* to good use. The Sceptics*—the only *honourable* type among the ever-so multiply ambiguous tribe of the philosophers!... Otherwise I resort almost always to the same books—basically a small number, of those books which have *proved* themselves for me in particular. It is perhaps not my nature to read much and widely: reading-rooms make me ill. It is also not my nature to love much or widely. Circumspection, even hostility towards new books is more of an instinct with me than 'tolerance', 'largeur du coeur',* and other kinds of 'brotherly love'... A small number of older Frenchmen are basically the ones I return to again and again: I believe only in French education and consider everything else that calls itself 'education' in Europe a misunderstanding, not to speak of German education... The few cases of advanced education I discovered in Germany were all of French extraction, above all Frau Cosima Wagner, by far the foremost voice in questions of taste that I have heard... The fact that I don't read Pascal but *love* him, as Christianity's most instructive sacrifice— slowly murdered, first physically, then psychologically, the whole logic of this most gruesome form of inhuman cruelty—the fact that I have something of Montaigne's mischief in my spirit—who knows? perhaps in my body, too—the fact that my artist's taste stands up for the names of Molière, Corneille, and Racine not without indignation against a wild genius like Shakespeare: in the last resort this does not stop me finding even the very latest Frenchmen charming company. I quite fail to see in what century in history one could fish out such curious yet delicate psychologists as in the Paris of today: I can name, to take a few examples—for they are by no means small in number—Messrs Paul Bourget, Pierre Loti, Gyp,* Meilhac, Anatole France, Jules Lemaître, or to highlight one of the strong race, a true Latin of whom I am especially fond, Guy de Maupassant. Just between ourselves, I even prefer *this* generation to their great teachers, every last one of whom has been ruined by German philosophy: Mr Taine, for example, by Hegel, to whom he owes his misunderstanding of great people and periods. Everywhere Germany extends it *ruins* culture. Not till the War* was the spirit 'redeemed'* in France... Stendhal, one of the most beautiful coincidences in my life—for everything momentous in it was always propelled in my direction by chance, never by a recommendation—is utterly invaluable with his psychologist's anticipatory eye, with his grasp of what is real that reminds you of the proximity of that most real of men (*ex ungue Napoleonem*—*); finally, not least as an *honest* atheist, a rare species in France and almost impossible to find (Prosper Mérimée be praised)... Perhaps I am even a little envious of Stendhal? He robbed me of the best atheist joke, which was just made for me to tell: 'God's only excuse is that he doesn't exist'... I myself said somewhere:* what has been the greatest objection to existence so far? *God*...

4

I was given the most exalted conception of the lyric poet by *Heinrich Heine*. I seek in vain across all the realms of millennia for a music that is as sweet and passionate. He possessed that divine malice without which I am incapable of conceiving perfection—I measure the value of people and races according to how necessary it is for them to conceive of god and satyr as inseparable.—And how he handles German! Some day people will say that Heine and I were by far the foremost artists of the German language—incalculably far beyond everything mere Germans have done with it.—I must be intimately related to *Byron's* Manfred:* I found all these abysses in myself—at 13 I was ripe enough for this work. I have no words, just a look for those who, in the presence of Manfred, can dare to utter the word 'Faust'.* The Germans are *incapable* of any conception of greatness: witness Schumann.* I myself, incensed at this sugary Saxon, composed a counter-overture to *Manfred*, on which Hans von Bülow commented that he had never seen the like on manuscript paper, that it was a rape of Euterpe.*—If I seek my highest formula for *Shakespeare*, then I only ever find this: that he conceived the type of Caesar.* You cannot just guess that kind of thing—you either are it or you aren't. The great poet creates *only* by drawing on his own reality*—to the point where he can no longer stand his work afterwards... Once I have cast a glance at my *Zarathustra*, I walk up and down the room for half an hour, overpowered by unbearable cramps brought on by sobbing.—I know of no more heart-rending reading-matter than Shakespeare: what must a person have suffered if he needs to be a clown that badly!—Is Hamlet *understood*?* It is not doubt but *certainty* that drives you mad... But you need to be profound, abyss, philosopher to feel that way... We are all *afraid* of the truth... And, to make no bones about it: I am instinctively sure and certain that Lord Bacon is the originator, the animal-self-tormentor* of this uncanniest kind of literature: what do *I* care about the pitiable prattle of American muddle-heads and blockheads?* But the strength to achieve the most powerful realization of one's vision is not only compatible with the most powerful strength to act, to act monstrously, to commit crime*—*it positively requires it*... We know far from enough about Lord Bacon, the first realist in every great sense of the word, to know *what* all the things he did were, *what* he wanted, *what* he experienced... And the devil take you, my dear critics! Assuming I had baptized my *Zarathustra* with another's name, for instance that of Richard Wagner, then it would have taken more than two millennia's worth of acumen to guess that the author of *Human, All Too Human* is the visionary of *Zarathustra**...

5

Now that I am speaking of the relaxations in my life, I need to say
a word to express my gratitude for what has been by far my most
profound and cordial relaxation. Without a shadow of doubt this
was my intimate association with Richard Wagner. It would cost
me little to forsake the rest of my human relationships, but not
at any price would I part with the Tribschen* days from my life,
days of trust, of cheerfulness, of sublime coincidences—of *profound* moments... I do not know what experiences others have had
with Wagner: never a cloud passed across our skies.—And with
this I return to France once again—I have no reasons, just a con-
temptuous corner of my mouth left over for Wagnerians
et hoc genus omne,* who think they are doing Wagner an honour
by finding that he resembles *them*... The way I am—alien to
everything German in my most profound instincts, so that even
having a German near me slows down my digestion—my first
contact with Wagner was also the first sigh of relief in my life:
I felt and honoured him as a *foreign land*, as an opposite, as a
protest against all 'German virtues' incarnate. We who were children
in the miasma of the fifties are necessarily pessimistic about the
concept 'German'; we can be nothing else but revolutionaries—
we will never acknowledge a state of affairs where *the hypocrites*
are on top. It is a matter of complete indifference to me whether
they go under different guises nowadays, dress in scarlet and wear
hussars' uniforms... Well then! Wagner was a revolutionary—he
escaped from the Germans... As an *artist* one can have no other
home in Europe than Paris; the *délicatesse** in all five artistic senses
which Wagner's art presupposes, the finger for nuances, the psychological morbidity, is only to be found in Paris. Nowhere else has this
passion in questions of form, this seriousness in *mise-en-scène*—it
is the Parisian seriousness par excellence. No one in Germany has
any idea of the immense ambition that lives in the soul of a
Parisian artist. Germans are good-natured—Wagner was not in
the least good-natured... But I have already said quite enough (in
Beyond Good and Evil, 256)* about where Wagner belongs, who
are his closest relations: they are the late Romantics in France,

that high-flown and high-blown kind of artist like Delacroix, like Berlioz, with a *fond** of sickness, of incurability in their being, downright fanatics of *expressivity*, virtuosos through and through... Who was the very first *intelligent* follower of Wagner? Charles Baudelaire, who was also the first to understand Delacroix, that typical *décadent* in whom a whole generation of artists recognized themselves—he was perhaps also the last... What have I never forgiven Wagner? That he *condescended* to the Germans—that he became Reich German*... Everywhere Germany extends it *ruins* culture.—

6

All things considered, I could not have endured my youth without Wagner's music. For I was *condemned* to live among Germans. To escape from unbearable pressure you need hashish. Well then, I needed Wagner. Wagner is the counter-poison par excellence for everything German—but still a poison, I don't deny... From the moment there was a piano score of *Tristan*—my compliments, Herr von Bülow!*—I was a Wagnerian. Wagner's earlier works I saw as beneath me—still too vulgar, too 'German'... But even today I am searching for a work that is as dangerously fascinating, as terribly and sweetly infinite* as *Tristan*—in all the arts I search in vain. All the strangenesses of Leonardo da Vinci lose their mystique when the first note of *Tristan* is sounded. This work is unquestionably Wagner's *non plus ultra*; he recovered from it with the *Mastersingers* and the *Ring*.* Getting healthier—with a nature like Wagner that is a *retrograde step*... I consider it a first-rate stroke of luck to have lived at the right time and to have lived precisely among Germans, in order to be *ripe* for this work: so pronounced is the psychologist's curiosity in me. The world is poor for anyone who has never been sick enough for this 'hellish ecstasy': it is permitted, it is almost imperative to use a mystical formulation here. —I think I know better than anyone else the immensity of what Wagner can achieve, the fifty worlds of strange delights which no one but he had the wings to reach; and the way I am—strong enough to turn even the most dubious and dangerous things to my advantage and thus grow stronger—I call Wagner the greatest benefactor of my life. What makes us related, the fact that we have suffered more profoundly—from each other, too—than people of this century could possibly suffer, will for ever reconcile our names; and just as surely as Wagner is a mere misunderstanding among Germans, so am I and always will be.—Two centuries of psychological and artistic discipline *first*, my dear Teutons!... But that can't be caught up.—

7

—Let me say a little more for the most select of ears: what *I* really want from music. That it should be cheerful and profound, like an October afternoon. That it should be independent, lively, tender, a sweet little woman of treachery and grace... I shall never grant that a German could *know* what music is. What are called German musicians, the greatest in the van, are *foreigners*, Slavs, Croats, Italians, Dutchmen—or Jews; otherwise Germans of the strong race, *extinct* Germans like Heinrich Schütz, Bach, and Handel. I myself am still enough of a Pole* to give up the rest of music for Chopin: for three reasons I would make an exception of Wagner's *Siegfried Idyll*,* perhaps Liszt too, who is ahead of all other musicians when it comes to noble orchestral accents, and lastly everything that has grown up beyond the Alps—*this* side*... I would not know how to do without Rossini, still less *my* musical south, the music of my Venetian maestro Pietro Gasti.* And when I say beyond the Alps, I am really only saying Venice. Whenever I look for another word for music, I always find only the word 'Venice'. I can make no distinction between tears and music; I do not know how to imagine happiness, the *south*, without a shudder of timidity.

> By the bridge stood I
> Lately in the dusky night.
> From afar came singing:
> In golden drops it welled up
> Across the quivering expanse.

Gondolas, lights, music—
Drunkenly they swam out into the gloaming...

My soul, a stringed instrument,
Sang to itself, invisibly touched,
A barcarole in secret accompaniment,
Quivering in mottled bliss.
—Was anyone listening?...

8

In all this—in the choice of nourishment, place and climate,
relaxation—an instinct of self-preservation is in command,
expressed most unambiguously as an instinct of *self-defence*. Not
seeing many things, not hearing them, not allowing them to
approach you—first ruse, first proof that you are no accident but
a necessity. The current term for this instinct of self-defence is
taste. Its imperative commands you not only to say 'no' where
a 'yes' would be an act of 'selflessness', but to say *'no' as little as
possible*, too. To part with, depart from anything which requires
you to say 'no' time and again. The sense in this is that expenditure
on defence, even small amounts, when it becomes the rule, a habit,
entails an extraordinary and utterly needless impoverishment. Our
great expenditures are the most frequent little amounts. Fending
off, not allowing to approach, is an expense—let us make no mistake about this—a strength *wasted* on negative purposes. Just by
needing always to fend things off, you can grow so weak that you
cannot defend yourself any more.—Let us say I stepped out of
the house and found, instead of tranquil and aristocratic Turin,
small-town Germany: my instinct would have to close itself off so
as to repress everything forcing itself on it from this flattened and
cowardly world. Or if I found big-city Germany, this edifice of
vice where nothing grows, where everything, good and bad, is
dragged in. Would it not mean I would have to become a *hedge-
hog*?—But having quills is a waste, in fact a double luxury when you
are free to have no quills at all, but to be *open*-handed...

Another ruse and self-defence consists in *reacting as rarely as possible* and withdrawing from situations and conditions in which one would be condemned to hang one's 'freedom', one's initiative out to dry, so to speak, and become a mere reagent. Let me take as an analogy one's dealings with books. The scholar, who basically just 'skims' books—on a moderate day the classicist gets through roughly 200—ends up completely losing the ability to think for himself. If he does not skim, he does not think. He *responds* to a stimulus (—an idea he has read) when he thinks—he ends up just reacting. The scholar expends all his strength in saying 'yes' and 'no', in critiquing what has already been thought—he himself no longer thinks... The instinct for self-defence has been worn down in him; otherwise he would defend himself against books. The scholar—a *décadent.*—I have seen it with my own eyes: gifted, rich, and freely disposed natures 'read to rack and ruin' even in their thirties, just matches that need rubbing to emit sparks— 'thoughts'.—In the early morning at break of day, when you are at your freshest, at the dawning of your strength, to read a *book*— that is what I call depraved!— —

9

At this point I can no longer avoid giving the actual answer to the question of *how to become what you are*. And with this I touch on the master-stroke in the art of self-preservation—of *egoism*... For if you assume that your task, your destiny, the *fate* of your task lies considerably beyond the average measure, then no danger would be greater than facing up to yourself *with* this task. Becoming what you are presupposes that you have not the slightest inkling *what* you are. From this point of view even life's *mistakes* have their own sense and value, the temporary byways and detours, the delays, the 'modesties', the seriousness wasted on tasks which lie beyond *the* task. Here a great ruse, even the highest ruse can be expressed: where *nosce te ipsum** would be the recipe for decline, then forgetting yourself, *misunderstanding* yourself, belittling, constricting, mediocritizing yourself becomes good sense itself.

In moral terms: brotherly love, living for other people and things *can* be a preventative measure for maintaining the harshest selfishness. This is the exception, when—against my habit and conviction—I side with the 'selfless' drives: in this case they labour in the service of *egoism, self-discipline*.*—You need to keep the whole surface of consciousness—consciousness *is* a surface—untainted by any of the great imperatives. Beware even every great phrase, every great pose! With all of them the instinct risks 'understanding itself' too soon— —Meanwhile, in the depths, the organizing 'idea' with a calling to be master grows and grows—it begins to command, it slowly leads you *back* out of byways and detours, it prepares *individual* qualities and skills which will one day prove indispensable as means to the whole—it trains one by one all the *ancillary* capacities before it breathes a word about the dominant task, about 'goal', 'purpose', 'sense'.—Seen from this angle my life is simply miraculous. The task of *revaluing values* required perhaps more capacities than have ever dwelt together in one individual, above all contradictory capacities, too, without them being allowed to disturb or destroy one another. Hierarchy of capacities; distance; the art of separating without creating enemies; not conflating, not 'reconciling' anything; an immense multiplicity which is nevertheless the opposite of chaos—this was the precondition, the long, secret labour and artistry of my instinct. Its *higher concern* was so pronounced that I never even suspected what was growing within me—that all my abilities would one day suddenly *spring forth* ripe, in their ultimate perfection. I lack any memory of ever having exerted myself—there is no trace of a *struggle* evident in my life, I am the opposite of a heroic nature. 'Wanting' something, 'striving' for something, having in view a 'purpose', a 'wish'—I know nothing of this from experience. Even now, I look towards my future—a *distant* future!—as if it were a smooth sea: not a ripple of a desire. I have not the slightest wish for anything to be other than it is; I myself do not want to be different. But this is how I have always lived. I have never wished for anything. Someone who can say after forty-four years that he has never striven for *honours*, for *women*, for *money*!—Not that

I lacked them... Thus one day, for example, I was a university professor—never for one moment had I thought of anything like this, as I was only just 24.* In the same way, two years earlier, I found I was a philologist one day: in the sense that my teacher Ritschl wanted to have my *first* philological work, my beginning in every sense, to print in his *Rheinisches Museum** (*Ritschl*—I say this in admiration—the only scholar of genius I have ever set eyes on to this day. He possessed that agreeable corruption that distinguishes us Thuringians and makes even a German likeable—even to reach the truth we still prefer the roundabout routes. With these words I do not mean at all to underestimate my close compatriot, *clever* Leopold von Ranke*...)

10

At this point a great stock-taking is needed. People will ask me why I have talked about all these little and, according to conventional opinion, trivial things; they will argue that I am doing myself no favours, all the more so if I am destined to fulfil great tasks. Answer: these little things—nourishment, place, climate, relaxation, the whole casuistry of egoism—are incomparably more important than anything that has been considered important hitherto. This is precisely where one must start *relearning*. What humanity has hitherto deemed important are not even realities, but merely illusions, more strictly speaking *lies* born of the bad instincts of sick natures that are in the most profound sense harmful—all the concepts 'God', 'soul', 'virtue', 'sin', 'hereafter', 'truth', 'eternal life'... But people have looked for the greatness of human nature, its 'divinity', in them... All questions of politics, of social ordering, of upbringing have been thoroughly falsified because the most harmful people were considered great—because people were taught to despise the 'petty' things, by which I mean the fundamental matters of life itself... Our contemporary culture is ambivalent to the highest degree... The German Kaiser making a pact with the Pope,* as if the Pope did not represent mortal enmity against life!... What is being built today will not be standing in three years' time.—If I measure myself against what I *can* do, not to speak of what follows in my wake, an unprecedented overturning and rebuilding, then I can stake more of a claim than any other mortal to the word 'greatness'. If I now compare myself with those who have hitherto been honoured as *foremost* among men, then the difference is palpable. I do not even count these so-called 'foremost' as men at all—for me they are humanity's rejects, hideous combinations of illness and vindictive instincts: they are nothing but disastrous, fundamentally incurable monsters taking their revenge on life... I want to be the opposite of this: it is my privilege to have the highest sensitivity for all the signs of healthy instincts. There is not a single sickly trait in my character; even in times of grave illness I did not become sickly; you will not find a trace of fanaticism in my being. There is not one moment in my life where you will find any evidence of a presumptuous or histrionic attitude. The pathos of posturing has *no* part in greatness; anyone who needs postures at all is *false*... Beware of all picturesque people!—I found life easy, easiest, when it demanded the most difficult things of me. Anyone who saw me in the seventy days of this autumn, when, without interruption, I did nothing but first-rate things which no one will do after me—or before me*—with a sense of responsibility for all the millennia after me, will have noticed not a trace of tension in me, but rather an overflowing freshness and cheerfulness. I never felt more agreeable about eating, I never slept better.—I know of no other way of dealing with great tasks than by *playing*: as a sign of greatness this is an important precondition. The slightest constraint, a gloomy expression, some harsh tone in the throat—these are all objections to a person, so how much more do they count against his work!... You must have no nerves... *Suffering* from solitude is an objection, too—I have only ever suffered from 'multitude'... At an absurdly young age, when I was 7, I already knew that no human word would ever get through to me: did anyone ever see me distressed at this?—Nowadays I am still as affable to everyone, I am even full of praise for the lowliest: in all of this there is not a jot of arrogance, of secret contempt. *Anyone* I despise *senses* that he is despised by me: by my mere existence

I infuriate anything that has bad blood in its body... My formula for human greatness is *amor fati*:* not wanting anything to be different, not forwards, not backwards, not for all eternity. Not just enduring what is necessary, still less concealing it—all idealism is hypocrisy in the face of what is necessary—but *loving* it...

WHY I WRITE SUCH GOOD BOOKS

I

I am one thing, my writings are another.—At this point, before I speak of the writings themselves, let me touch on the question of their being understood or *not* understood. I'll do so as casually as is somehow appropriate: for this question is not at all timely. I myself am not yet timely; some are born posthumously.*—One day there will be a need for institutions in which people live and teach as I understand living and teaching; then, perhaps, they will even set up university chairs dedicated to the interpretation of *Zarathustra*. But I would be completely contradicting myself if today already I expected ears *and hands* for *my* truths: that people today don't hear, that people today don't know how to take from me, is not only comprehensible, it even seems to me to be right. I don't want to be mistaken for anyone—so I mustn't mistake myself.—To say it again,* there is little evidence in my life of 'ill will'; I scarcely know any case of literary 'ill will' to talk of, either. But there's too much evidence of *pure folly**... It strikes me as one of the rarest distinctions anyone can bestow on themselves when they pick up a book of mine; I am even assuming they take their shoes off to do so—not to speak of boots*... Once, when Dr Heinrich von Stein was complaining in all honesty that he didn't understand a word of my *Zarathustra*, I told him that that was as it should be: understanding—in other words *experiencing*— six sentences of it, raises you up to a higher level of mortals than 'modern' men could ever reach. With *this* feeling of distance, how *could* I even just want the 'moderns' I know to—read me! My triumph is precisely the opposite of Schopenhauer's—I say *'non legor, non legar'*.*—Not that I would want to underestimate the pleasure I often had from the *innocence* with which people said 'no' to my writings. Just this summer, at a time when with my weighty, over-weighty literature I was perhaps capable of throwing off balance all the rest of literature, a professor from Berlin University kindly gave me to understand that I really should use another form: no one reads that kind of thing.—In the end it wasn't Germany but Switzerland that has provided the two extreme cases. An essay by Dr V. Widmann in *Bund*, on *Beyond Good and Evil*, entitled 'Nietzsche's Dangerous Book', and a review article on all my books by Karl Spitteler, again in *Bund*,* are a maximum in my life—of what, I am careful not to say... The latter treated my *Zarathustra*, for example, as a 'higher stylistic exercise', and wished that I might later see to the content, too; Dr Widmann expressed his respect for the courage with which I was striving to abolish all decent feelings.—By a little quirk of chance every sentence here, with a logical consistency I admired, was a truth turned on its head: basically all you had to do was 'revalue all the values' to hit the nail on the head about me in a quite remarkable way—instead of hitting my head with a nail... All the more reason to attempt an explanation.—Ultimately no one can hear in things—books included—more than he already knows. If you have no access to something from experience, you will have no ear for it. Now let us imagine an extreme case, where a book tells only of experiences which it is quite impossible to have often or even just rarely—where it is the *first* to speak for a new series of experiences. In this case simply nothing will be heard, with the acoustic illusion that where nothing is heard *nothing is there, either*... Ultimately this is my average experience and, if you will, the *originality* of my experience. Those who thought they understood me have turned me into something else, in their own image*—not uncommonly into an opposite of me, for instance an 'idealist'; those who understood nothing of me denied I was even worth considering.—The word '*overman*'* as a designation for the type that has turned out best, by contrast with 'modern' men, 'good' men, Christians and other nihilists—a word which, in the mouth of a Zarathustra, the *destroyer* of morality, becomes a very thought-provoking word—has been understood almost everywhere, in all innocence, in the sense of those values whose opposite was made manifest in the figure of Zarathustra, in other words as the 'idealistic' type of a higher kind of man, half 'saint', half 'genius'... It has led some scholarly blockheads to suspect me of Darwinism;*

people have recognized in it even the 'hero cult' of that great unknowing and reluctant counterfeiter, Carlyle, which I have been so malicious as to reject.* If I whispered in someone's ear that they should look around for a Cesare Borgia rather than a Parsifal,* they didn't believe their ears.—You will have to forgive me for not being in the slightest curious about reviews of my books, especially in newspapers. My friends, my publishers know about this and don't talk to me of such things. In one particular case I once set eyes on all the sins that had been committed against a specific book—it was *Beyond Good and Evil*—I'd have some charming things to report about that. Can you believe it, that the *Nationalzeitung*—a Prussian newspaper, let us note for my foreign readers; I myself, with respect, read only the *Journal des Débats**—thought fit to see the book, in all seriousness, as a 'sign of the times', as the true and authentic *Junker philosophy*, for which the *Kreuzzeitung** lacked only the courage?...

2

That was said for the benefit of Germans: for I have readers everywhere else—nothing but the *choicest* intelligences, proven characters raised in high positions and duties; I even have true geniuses among my readers. In Vienna, in St Petersburg, in Stockholm, in Copenhagen, in Paris and New York—I have been discovered everywhere: *except* in Europe's flatland Germany... And, to admit it openly, I am even more pleased about my non-readers, those who have never heard my name or the word 'philosophy'; but wherever I come to, here in Turin for instance, everyone's face lights up and softens when they see me. What I have found most flattering so far is that old women pedlars don't rest till they have found their sweetest grapes for me. *That's how far* you need to take being a philosopher... Not for nothing are the Poles called the French among the Slavs.* Not for a moment will a charming Russian woman get confused over where I belong. I just can't be solemn—it's as much as I can manage to be embarrassed... Thinking in a German way, feeling in a German way—I can do anything, but *that* is beyond me... My old teacher

Ritschl went so far as to claim that I conceived even my philological treatises as a Parisian *romancier** would—in an absurdly exciting manner. In Paris itself people are astounded at 'toutes mes audaces et finesses'* (the expression is from Monsieur Taine) I am afraid that you will find mixed into my writings, right up to the most exalted forms of the dithyramb, a little of that salt that never turns stupid, 'German'—*esprit**... I can do no other. God help me! Amen.*—We all know what a long-ears is, some even know it from experience. Well then, I make so bold as to assert that I have the tiniest ears. This is of no little interest to the little women—it seems to me that they feel better understood by me?... I am the *anti-ass* par excellence and hence a world-historic monster—I am, in Greek, and not only in Greek, the *Antichrist*...

3

I know my prerogatives as a writer to some extent; in certain cases I even have evidence of how much it 'ruins' people's taste if they get used to my writings. They simply can no longer stand other books, least of all philosophy books. It is an unparalleled distinction to step into this noble and delicate world—for which you must not on any account be a German; ultimately it is a distinction you need to have earned. But anyone who is related to me through the *loftiness* of their willing experiences true ecstasies of learning when they do: for I come from heights to which no bird has yet flown, I know abysses into which no foot has yet strayed. I have been told it is not possible to let a book of mine out of one's hands—that I even disturb people's sleep... There is definitely no prouder and at the same time more refined kind of book: here and there they achieve the highest thing that can be achieved on earth, cynicism; you must tackle them with the most delicate fingers as well as with the bravest fists. Every infirmity of the soul rules you out, once and for all, even every attack of indigestion: you must have no nerves, you must have a cheerful abdomen. Not only the poverty of a soul but its cramped air rules you out, and all the more so anything cowardly, unclean, secretly vengeful in the intestines: one word from me drives out all the bad instincts.

I have several guinea-pigs among my acquaintances who allow me
to indulge myself in the various—very instructively various—
reactions to my writings. Those who want nothing to do with their
contents, for example my so-called friends, become 'impersonal':
they congratulate me on having 'done it' again—and they claim
I have made progress with my more cheerful tone... The utterly
depraved 'spirits', the 'beautiful souls',* the hypocritical through
and through, have absolutely no idea where to begin with these
books—so they consider them to be *beneath* them, the beautiful
logical consistency of all 'beautiful souls'. The blockheads among
my acquaintances—mere Germans, if you'll excuse my saying
so—give me to understand that they don't always share my opinion, but now and then, for example... I have heard this said even
about *Zarathustra*... Likewise any 'femininism'* in people, including men, bars the way to me: they will never enter this labyrinth of
daring knowledge. You must never have spared yourself, you must
have become accustomed to *harshness* to feel high-spirited and
cheerful among nothing but harsh truths. If I conjure up the image
of a perfect reader, it always turns into a monster of courage and
curiosity, and what's more something supple, cunning, cautious,
a born adventurer and discoverer. Ultimately if I am to say who
are basically the only people I am speaking to, I can't put it any
better than did Zarathustra. *Who* are the only people he wants to
tell his riddle to?

> To you, bold searchers, tempters, experimenters,* and who-
> ever has embarked with cunning sails upon terrifying seas—
> to you, who are drunk with riddles, glad of twilight, whose
> souls are lured with flutes to every confounding chasm:
> —for you do not want to grope along a thread with cowardly
> hand;* and, where you can *guess*, you hate to *deduce*...

4

At the same time I'll say something about my *art of style* in general.
Communicating a state, an inner tension of pathos through signs,
including the tempo of these signs—that is the point of every

style; and considering that in my case the multiplicity of inner states is extraordinary, in my case there are many stylistic possibilities—altogether the most multifarious art of style anyone has ever had at their disposal. Every style is *good* that really communicates an inner state, that makes no mistake with signs, with the tempo of signs, with *gestures*—all laws governing the rhetorical period are an art of gesture. Here my instinct is infallible.—Good style *in itself*—*pure folly*,* mere 'idealism' like, for instance, the 'beautiful *in itself*', like the 'good *in itself*', like the 'thing *in itself*'... Always assuming that there are ears—that there are those who are capable and worthy of such a pathos, that those to whom one *may* communicate oneself are not lacking.—My Zarathustra, for example, is still looking for such people in the meantime—oh, he will need to look for a long time yet!—You must be *worthy* of hearing him... And till then there will be no one to understand the *art* that has been squandered here: no one has ever had more new, unprecedented artistic means to squander—means really created only for this purpose. That such a thing was possible in German, of all languages, remained to be proven: I myself would have denied it beforehand in the harshest possible terms. Before me, people did not know what can be done with the German language—what can be done with language *tout court*.—The art of *grand* rhythm, the *grand style* of the period expressing an immense rise and fall of sublime, superhuman* passion was first discovered by me; with a dithyramb like the last in the Third Part of *Zarathustra*, entitled 'The Seven Seals', I flew a thousand miles beyond what had hitherto been called poetry.

5

—The fact that from my writings there speaks a *psychologist* beyond compare, this is perhaps the first insight a good reader achieves—a reader such as I deserve, who reads me as good old philologists used to read their Horace. The principles which in essence are commonly agreed upon by all—not to speak of the common or garden philosophers,* the moralists and other hollow-pots, cabbage-heads*—appear in my writings as naive misconceptions: for example the belief that 'unegoistic' and 'egoistic' are opposites, when the ego itself is just a 'higher swindle', an 'ideal'... There are *no* egoistic *or* unegoistic actions: both concepts are psychological absurdities. Or the principle 'man strives for happiness'... Or the principle 'happiness is virtue's reward'... Or the principle 'pleasure and displeasure are opposites'... The Circe* of humanity, morality, has falsified beyond recognition—*infected*—all *psychologica*,* right down to that ghastly nonsense, that love should be something 'unegoistic'... You have to be sure of *yourself*, you have to be standing bravely on your own two feet, otherwise you simply *cannot* love. The little women know that only too well, after all: they don't give a damn about selfless, merely objective men... May I venture the supposition, by the by, that I *know* the little women? That is an aspect of my Dionysian dowry. Who knows? perhaps I am the foremost psychologist of the eternal feminine.* They all love me—an old story: excluding the *botched* little women, the 'emancipated' ones, who are incapable of producing children.—Fortunately I am not willing to let myself be torn apart: the perfect woman tears apart when she loves... I know these charming maenads*... Ah, what dangerous, insidious, subterranean little predators! And so pleasant with it!... A little woman running after her revenge would run down fate itself.— Woman is unutterably more wicked than man, and cleverer; goodness in a woman is already a form of *degeneration*... Deep down inside all so-called 'beautiful souls'* there is a physiological illness—I shan't say any more, to avoid becoming medicynical. The struggle for *equal* rights is even a symptom of illness: every doctor knows that.—The more womanly a woman is, the more she fights tooth and nail to defend herself against any kind of rights: the natural state, the eternal *war* between the sexes puts her in first place by a wide margin, after all.—Did anyone have ears for my definition of love? it is the only one worthy of a philosopher. Love—war in its means, at bottom the deadly hatred of the sexes.*—Did anyone hear my answer to the question of how you *cure*—'redeem'—a woman? You get her pregnant. Woman needs children, man is always just a means: thus spoke Zarathustra.*—'Emancipation of woman'—this is the instinctual hatred of the *botched*, i.e. infertile woman against the woman who turned out well—the struggle against 'men' is always just a means, a pretext, a tactic. By raising *themselves* up—as 'woman in herself', as 'higher woman', as 'idealist' of a woman*—they want to bring *down* the general level of woman's standing; nothing is more guaranteed to achieve this than high-school education, trousers, and the right to vote like political cattle. The emancipated ones are basically the *anarchists* in the world of the 'eternal feminine', the ones who turned out badly, whose nethermost instinct is for revenge... An entire species of the most malignant 'idealism'— which can be found, incidentally, in men, too, for example in Henrik Ibsen, that typical old maid—aims to *poison* the good conscience, what is natural in sexual love... And so as to leave no doubts about my views, which in this respect are as honourable as they are strict, I want to share one more principle from my moral code against *vice*: with the word 'vice' I am combating every kind of anti-nature* or, if you like pretty words, idealism. The principle runs thus: 'preaching chastity is a public incitement to perversity. All despising of the sexual life, all besmirching of it by calling it "impure" is the crime of crimes against life—it is the true sin against the holy spirit of life.'*—

6

To give an idea of myself as psychologist, I'll take a curious piece of psychology that appears in *Beyond Good and Evil*—incidentally I forbid any speculation as to whom I am describing here. 'The genius of the heart, a heart of the kind belonging to that great secretive one, the tempter god and born Pied Piper of the conscience whose voice knows how to descend into the underworld of every soul, who does not utter a word or send a glance without its having a crease and aspect that entices, whose mastery consists in part in knowing how to seem—and seem not what he is, but rather what those who follow him take as one *more* coercion to press ever closer to him, to follow him ever more inwardly and completely... The genius of the heart that silences everything loud and self-satisfied and teaches it how to listen; that smooths out rough souls and gives them a taste of a new longing (to lie still, like a mirror, so that the deep sky can mirror itself upon them)... The genius of the heart, that teaches the foolish and over-hasty hand to hesitate and to grasp more daintily; that guesses the hidden and forgotten treasure, the drop of kindness and sweet spirituality lying under thick, turbid ice and is a divining rod for every speck of gold that has long lain buried in some dungeon of great mud and sand... The genius of the heart, from whose touch everyone goes forth the richer, neither reprieved nor surprised, not as if delighted or depressed by another's goodness, but rather richer in themselves, newer than before, opened up, breathed upon and sounded out by a warm wind, more unsure, perhaps, more brooding, breakable, broken, but full of hopes that still remain nameless, full of new willing and streaming, full of new not-willing and back-streaming...'*

The Birth of Tragedy

I

To be fair to *The Birth of Tragedy* (1872), several things will have to be forgotten. It owed its *impact* and even its fascination to what was wrong with it—its tactical use of *Wagnerism*, as if that were a symptom of *ascent*. This is precisely why the work was an event in Wagner's life: only then did Wagner's name start to conjure up great hopes. People still remind me of it even today, maybe in the midst of *Parsifal*:* blaming *me* for the fact that such a high opinion of the *cultural value* of this movement gained the ascendancy. —Several times I have found the work cited as *The Rebirth of Tragedy out of the Spirit of Music*: people had ears only for a new formulation of *Wagner's* art, his aim, his *task*—and thus they failed to hear the fundamentally valuable things the work was hiding. *Hellenism and Pessimism*: that would have been a more unambiguous title:* in other words as the first explanation of how the Greeks coped with pessimism—by what means they *overcame* it... Tragedy is precisely the proof that the Greeks were *no* pessimists: Schopenhauer was wrong about this, as he was wrong about everything.*—If you pick up *The Birth of Tragedy* with some degree of neutrality, it looks very untimely: you would never dream that it was *begun* amidst the thunder of the Battle of Woerth.* I thought through these problems outside the walls of Metz, on cold September nights, in the midst of serving as a medical orderly; you might easily think the work was fifty years older. It is politically indifferent—'un-German' in today's parlance—it smells offensively Hegelian, and in just a few phrases it is tainted with the doleful scent of Schopenhauer. An 'idea'—the Dionysian/Apollonian opposition—translated into metaphysics, history itself as the development of this 'idea'; in tragedy the opposition sublated to become a unity;* from this point of view things that had never looked each other in the face before suddenly juxtaposed, illuminated, and *understood* in the light of each other... Opera, for instance, and revolution*... The book's two decisive *innovations* are, on the one hand, its understanding of the *Dionysian* phenomenon among the Greeks—it provides the first psychology of it and sees it as the single root of all Greek art—and on the other hand its understanding of Socratism: Socrates recognized for the first time as the instrument of Greek dissolution, as a typical *décadent*. 'Rationality' *against* instinct. 'Rationality' at any price as a dangerous, life-undermining power!*—Profound, hostile silence about Christianity throughout the book. It is neither Apollonian nor Dionysian; it *negates* all *aesthetic* values—the only values *The Birth of Tragedy* recognizes— it is in the most profound sense nihilistic, whereas in the Dionysian symbol the outermost limit of *affirmation* is reached. At one point there is an allusion to Christian priests as a 'spiteful kind of dwarves', of 'subterraneans'*...

2

This beginning is utterly remarkable. I had *discovered* the only analogy for and counterpart to my innermost experience that history has to offer—at the same time I was the first to understand the marvellous phenomenon of the Dionysian.* Likewise my recognizing Socrates as a *décadent* provided wholly unambiguous proof of how little the assuredness of my psychological grasp was in danger from any moral idiosyncrasy—morality itself as a symptom of *décadence* is an innovation, a first-rate one-off in the history of knowledge. With these two things, how high had I leapt above the pitiful blockhead-chatter of optimism versus pessimism!— I was the first to see the real opposition—*degenerating* instinct turning against life with subterranean vengefulness (—its typical forms Christianity, the philosophy of Schopenhauer, to a certain extent the philosophy of Plato already, all idealism) and a formula, born of abundance, superabundance, for the *highest affirmation*, a yes-saying without reservation, even to suffering, even to guilt, even to everything questionable and alien about existence... This latter, the most joyful, most effusively high-spirited 'yes' to life, is not only the highest insight, it is also the *most profound*, the one which is most rigorously confirmed and sustained by truth and science. Nothing that is can be discounted, nothing can be dispensed with—indeed, the aspects of existence that are rejected by Christians and other nihilists occupy an infinitely higher place in the hierarchy of values than what the *décadence* instinct has seen fit to sanction, to *call 'good'*.* To understand this requires *courage* and, as its prerequisite, a surplus of *strength*: for one comes only so close to truth as one's strength *allows* one's courage to dare advance. Knowledge, saying 'yes' to reality, is just as much a necessity for the strong as are, for the weak (inspired by weakness), cowardice and *flight* from reality—the 'ideal'... They are not free to know: *décadents need* the lie, it is one of the conditions of their preservation. —Anyone who not only understands the word 'Dionysian' but understands *himself* in the word 'Dionysian' has no need for a refutation of Plato or Christianity or Schopenhauer—he can *smell the decay*...

3

The extent to which, with this, I had found the concept of 'tragic', the ultimate knowledge of what the psychology of tragedy is, was given expression recently in *Twilight of the Idols*: 'Saying yes to life, even in its strangest and hardest problems; the will to life rejoicing in the *sacrifice* of its highest types to its own inexhaustibility—*this* is what I called Dionysian, *this* is what I understood as a bridge to the psychology of the *tragic* poet. *Not* freeing oneself from terror and pity, not purging oneself of a dangerous emotion through a vehement discharge—such was Aristotle's misunderstanding of it*—but, over and above terror and pity, *being oneself* the eternal joy of becoming, that joy which also encompasses the *joy of destruction*...'* In this sense I have the right to see myself as the first *tragic philosopher*—which means the polar opposite and antipodes of a pessimistic philosopher. Before me one doesn't find this transformation of the Dionysian into a philosophical pathos: *tragic wisdom* is lacking—I have looked in vain for signs of it even among the *great* philosophical Greeks, those who lived in the two centuries *before* Socrates.* I had a lingering doubt about *Heraclitus*, in whose vicinity I feel altogether warmer, better disposed than anywhere else. The affirmation of transience *and destruction*, the decisive feature of any Dionysian philosophy, saying 'yes' to opposition and war, *becoming*, with a radical rejection of even the concept of 'being'— in this I must in any event acknowledge ideas that are more closely related to mine than any that have hitherto been thought. The doctrine of the 'eternal recurrence', in other words of the unconditional and infinitely repeated circulation of all things—ultimately this doctrine of Zarathustra's *could* also have been taught already by Heraclitus. At least the Stoics, who inherited almost all their fundamental ideas from Heraclitus, show traces of it.*—

4

Out of this work speaks an immense hope. Ultimately I have no reason to retract my hope in a Dionysian future for music. Let us glance ahead a century, and let us suppose that my attack on two millennia of perversity and defilement of the human has been successful. That new party of life which takes in hand the greatest of all tasks, the breeding of a higher humanity, including the ruthless destruction of everything degenerating and parasitic, will make possible again that *excess of life* on earth from which the Dionysian state, too, must arise once again. I promise a *tragic* age: the highest art of saying 'yes' to life, tragedy, will be reborn once humanity has put behind it the awareness of the harshest but most necessary wars, *without suffering from it*... A psychologist might add that what I heard in Wagnerian music in my youth has nothing whatsoever to do with Wagner; that when I was describing Dionysian music I was describing what *I* had heard—that I instinctively had to translate and transfigure everything into the new spirit I bore inside me. The proof of this, *as strong a proof as any can be*, is my work *Wagner in Bayreuth*:* in all the psychologically decisive passages it speaks of me alone—one can ruthlessly put my name or the word 'Zarathustra' wherever the text has the word 'Wagner'. The whole picture of the *dithyrambic* artist is the picture of the *Zarathustra* poet *pre-existing*, sketched in with abyssal profundity and without even touching on the Wagnerian reality for a moment. Wagner himself had an inkling of this; he failed to recognize himself in the work.— Likewise 'the Bayreuth idea' had been transformed into something which will be no mystery to those who know my *Zarathustra*: into that *great noon-day*,* when the most select dedicate themselves to the greatest of all tasks—who knows? the vision of a celebration I have yet to experience... The pathos of the opening pages is world-historic; the *gaze* which is mentioned on page 7* is the true gaze of Zarathustra; Wagner, Bayreuth, all the petty German wretchedness is a cloud in which an unending *fata morgana** of the future is reflected. Even psychologically all the decisive traits of my own nature are invested in Wagner's—the juxtaposition of the most lucid and most fateful energies, the will to power such as no man has ever possessed it, ruthless bravery in intellectual matters, boundless energy to learn without it stifling the will to act. Everything about this work is anticipatory: the closeness of the return of the Greek spirit, the necessity of *Anti-Alexanders* to re*tie* the Gordian knot of Greek culture after it was undone*... Just listen to the world-historic emphasis with which, on page 30,* the concept of 'tragic cast of mind' is introduced: there are nothing but world-historic emphases in this work. This is the strangest kind of 'objectivity' there can be: an absolute certainty about what I *am* was projected onto a chance reality—the truth about myself spoke from a terrifying depth. On page 71* Zarathustra's *style* is described and anticipated with trenchant assuredness; and you will never find a more magnificent expression of the *event* that is Zarathustra, the immense act of purifying and consecrating humanity, than is found on pages 43–6.*—

The Untimelies

I

The four *Untimelies** are thoroughly warlike. They prove that
I was no daydreamer with his head in the clouds, that it gives me
pleasure to draw my rapier—perhaps also that I am dangerously
dexterous. The *first* attack (1873)* was aimed at German education,
which at that stage I was already looking down on with merciless
contempt. No point, no substance, no goal: mere 'public opinion'.
No more pernicious misunderstanding than to think that the
Germans' great military success provided any evidence at all in
favour of this education—let alone *its* victory over France… The
second Untimely (1874)* highlights what is dangerous about our
kind of scientific endeavour, what there is in it that gnaws away at
life and poisons it—life made *ill* by this dehumanized machinery
and mechanism, by the '*im*personality' of the worker, by the false
economy of the 'division of labour'. The *end*, culture, is lost—the
means, modern scientific endeavour, *barbarizes*… In this essay the
'historical sense', in which this century takes pride, was recognized
for the first time as an illness, as a typical sign of decay.—In the
third and *fourth Untimelies*,* however, as hints towards a *higher*
conception of culture, towards the restoration of the concept
'culture', two images of the harshest *egoism*, *self-discipline** are set
up, untimely types par excellence, full of sovereign contempt for
everything around them called 'Reich', 'education', 'Christianity',
'Bismarck', 'success'—Schopenhauer and Wagner *or*, in one word,
Nietzsche…

2

Of these four attacks the first was extraordinarily successful. The
uproar it prompted was in every sense magnificent. I had touched
on a triumphant nation's sore point—that its triumph was *not* a
cultural event but perhaps, perhaps, something quite different…

The response came from all sides and by no means just from the old friends of David Strauss, whom I had ridiculed as the type of German-educated philistinism and smugness, in short as the author of his barstool-gospel of the 'old faith and the new'* (—the phrase 'educated philistine' entered the language through my essay).* These old friends, Württembergers and Swabians whom I had dealt a mortal blow by finding their weird and wonderful animal Strauss funny, responded as worthily and coarsely as I could have wished; the Prussian retorts were cleverer—they had more 'Prussian blue'* in them. The greatest indecency was perpetrated by a Leipzig paper, the infamous *Grenzboten*;* I had difficulty preventing the outraged Baselers from taking steps. Only a few old men came out unequivocally on my side, for various and to some extent inscrutable reasons. Among them was Ewald in Göttingen, who intimated that my attack had been the death of Strauss.* Likewise the old Hegelian Bruno Bauer,* who from then on was one of my most attentive readers. In his last years he loved making references to me, for example giving Herr von Treitschke, the Prussian historian, a tip about whose work he could turn to to find out about the concept of 'culture', which had escaped him. The most thoughtful and also the most extensive comments on the work and its author came from a former pupil of the philosopher von Baader, a Professor Hoffmann in Würzburg. He foresaw in the work a great destiny for me—ushering in a kind of crisis and highest decision for the problem of atheism, whose most instinctive and ruthless type he guessed I was. Atheism was what led me to Schopenhauer.—By far the best heard, the most bitterly felt was an extraordinarily strong and brave recommendation from the otherwise so unassuming Karl Hillebrand, the last *humane* German to wield a pen. His essay was read in the *Augsburger Zeitung*; you can read it today, in a somewhat more cautious form, in his collected writings.* Here the work was presented as an event, a turning-point, a first self-contemplation, the best sign of all, as a real *return* of German seriousness and German passion in spiritual matters. Hillebrand was full of high praise for the form of the work, for its mature taste, for its perfect tact in

distinguishing man and matter: he marked it out as the best
polemical work ever written in German—in the art of polemic
which for Germans above all is so dangerous, so inadvisable.
Unreservedly affirmative, even intensifying what I had dared say
about the linguistic dilapidation in Germany (—nowadays they
are playing the purists* and can no longer construct a sentence—),
with the same contempt for the 'premier writers' of this nation, he
ended by expressing his admiration for my *courage*—that 'highest
form of courage that puts the very darlings of a people in the
dock'... The after-effects of this piece have been absolutely invaluable in my life. No one has yet picked a quarrel with me. In Germany
people keep quiet, they treat me with a gloomy caution: for years
I have made use of an absolute freedom of speech for which no
one nowadays, least of all in the 'Reich', has a free enough *hand*.
For me, paradise is 'beneath the shade of my sword'... Basically
I had put into practice one of Stendhal's maxims:* his advice is to
make one's entry into society with a *duel*. And what an opponent
I had chosen for myself! the first German free-thinker!... In fact
a completely *new* kind of free-thinking was finding its first expression here: to this day nothing is more alien and unrelated to me than
the whole European and American species of 'libres penseurs'.*
I am even more profoundly at odds with these incorrigible blockheads and buffoons, with their 'modern ideas', than I am with any
of their opponents. They, too, want to 'improve' humanity in their
way, in their image; they would wage implacable war on what I am,
what I *want*, if they only understood it—to a man they all still
believe in the 'ideal'... I am the first *immoralist*—

3

I would not want to claim that the two *Untimelies* that bear the
names of Schopenhauer and Wagner might be any particular help
in understanding or even just psychologically questioning the two
cases—except in one or two respects, as is only proper. Thus, for
example, with a profound instinctual assuredness what is elemental
in Wagner's nature is already described here as a histrionic talent

which is simply being logically consistent in its means and aims. With these works I basically wanted to do something quite different from psychology—an unparalleled problem of education, a new concept of *self-discipline*, of *self-defence* to the point of harshness, a path to greatness and to world-historic tasks was clamouring for its first expression. Broadly speaking I seized two famous and still utterly undetermined types with both hands, as you seize an opportunity with both hands, in order to express something, to have a few more formulations, signs, linguistic means in hand. After all, with quite uncanny sagacity the third *Untimely* also indicates this on p. 93.* This is how Plato used Socrates, as a semiotic for Plato. —Now that I am looking back from some distance on the circumstances to which these works bear witness, I would not want to deny that they basically speak only of me. The work *Wagner in Bayreuth* is a vision of my future, while *Schopenhauer as Educator* bears my innermost history, my *becoming* inscribed within it. Above all my *vow*!... *What* I am today, *where* I am today—at a height where I no longer speak with words but with lightning bolts—oh how far away I still was then!—But I could *see* the land*—not for one moment did I deceive myself about the path, sea, danger—*and* success! The great calmness in promising, this blessed peering out into a future which is not to remain a mere promise!—Here every word is experienced, profound, inward; there is no lack of the most painful things, there are words in here that are positively bloodthirsty. But a wind of *great* freedom blows across everything; even the wound does *not* serve as an objection.—How I understand the philosopher, as a terrible explosive which puts everything in danger,* how I set my concept of 'philosopher' miles apart from a concept which includes even a Kant, not to speak of the academic 'ruminants' and other professors of philosophy: this work gives invaluable instruction in all this, even granted that it is basically not 'Schopenhauer as Educator' but his *opposite*, 'Nietzsche as Educator', who is given a chance to speak here.—Considering that mine was a scholar's trade at the time, and perhaps that I *understood* my trade, too, then an austere aspect of the psychology of the scholar that suddenly comes to light in this work is not without significance: it expresses the *feeling of distance*, the profound certainty about what in me can be my *task*, what merely my means, intermission, and incidental accomplishment. It is my kind of cleverness to have been many things and in many places, so as to be able to become one thing—to be able to come to one thing. I *had* to be a scholar, too, for a while.—

Human, All Too Human
With Two Continuations

I

Human, All Too Human is the monument to a crisis. It calls itself a book for *free* spirits:* practically every sentence in it expresses a victory—with it I liberated myself from what in my nature *did not belong to me*. Idealism does not belong to me: the title says 'where *you* see ideal things, *I* see—human, oh just all-too-human things!'... I know man *better*... —There is no other way for the phrase 'free spirit' to be understood here: a spirit that has *become free*, that has seized possession of itself again. The tone, the timbre is completely different: people will find the book clever, cool, perhaps harsh and mocking. A certain intellectuality of *noble* taste seems to be continually keeping the upper hand over a more passionate current beneath it. In this context it makes sense that it is actually the hundredth anniversary of the death of *Voltaire* which provides the excuse, so to speak, for the publication of this book as early as 1878.* For Voltaire, in contrast with everyone who wrote after him, is above all a *grandseigneur** of the spirit: precisely what I am, too.—The name Voltaire on a work of mine— that really was progress—*towards myself*... If you look more closely, then you discover a merciless spirit who knows all the hiding-places where the ideal has its home—where it has its dungeons and its last safe retreat, as it were. With a torch in its hands casting an unwaver- ing light, with piercing brightness it illuminates this *underworld* of the ideal. It is war, but war without powder or smoke, with no war- like poses, no pathos or contorted limbs—all this would itself still be 'idealism'. One error after another is calmly put on ice; the ideal is not refuted—*it dies of exposure*... Here, for example, 'the genius' is freezing; a *long way* further on freezes 'the saint'; beneath a thick icicle 'the hero' is freezing; in the end 'belief', so-called 'conviction' freezes, even 'pity' is growing considerably cooler—almost every- where 'the thing in itself' is freezing to death...

2

The beginnings of this book can be found amid the weeks of
the first Bayreuth Festival;* a profound sense of alienation from
everything that surrounded me there was one of its preconditions.
Anyone who has an idea of the kind of visions that had already
crossed my path by that stage can guess how I felt when I woke
up one day in Bayreuth. Just as if I was dreaming... But where
was I? I recognized nothing, I hardly recognized Wagner. I leafed
through my memories in vain. Tribschen—a distant isle of the
blest: not the slightest similarity. The incomparable days of the
laying of the foundation stone,* the little group who *belonged*
there, who celebrated it and on whom you did not have first to
wish the fingers for delicate things: not the slightest similarity.
What had happened?—They had translated Wagner into German!
The Wagnerian had become master over Wagner!—*German* art!
the *German* master! *German* beer!... We others, who know only
too well the refined artists, the cosmopolitanism of taste to which
only Wagner's art speaks, were beside ourselves at finding Wagner
decked out with German 'virtues'.—I think I know the Wagnerian,
I have 'experienced' three generations, starting with the late Brendel,
who confused Wagner with Hegel, and going right up to the
'idealists' of the *Bayreuther Blätter*,* who confuse Wagner with
themselves—I have heard all kinds of confessions of 'beautiful
souls' about Wagner. A kingdom for one sensible word!*—A truly
hair-raising group! Nohl, Pohl, *Kohl* with grace ad infinitum!* No
deformity lacking from their number, not even the anti-Semite.
—Poor Wagner! Where had he ended up!—If he had only gone
among swine,* at least! But among Germans!... For the instruction of posterity they ought finally to stuff a genuine Bayreuther,
better still embalm him in spirit, for spirit is what's lacking—with
the caption: this is what the 'spirit' looked like on which the 'Reich'
was founded... Enough: in the midst of all this I headed off for a
few weeks, very suddenly, despite the fact that a charming Parisian
woman* tried to console me; I made my excuses to Wagner with
just a fatalistic telegram. In a spot buried away deep in the Bavarian
Forest, Klingenbrunn, I carried my melancholy and contempt for

Germans around with me like an illness—*and* wrote a sentence in my notebook from time to time, under the general heading of 'The Ploughshare', nothing but *harsh psychologica*, which can perhaps still be rediscovered in *Human, All Too Human*.

3

The decision that was taking shape in me at that time was not just a break with Wagner—I was registering a general aberration of my instinct, and individual mistakes, whether Wagner or my professorship in Basle, were only a sign. I was overcome by an *impatience* with myself; I realized it was high time to reflect on *myself*. All at once it became terribly clear to me how much time had already been wasted—how useless, how arbitrary my whole philologist's existence appeared when set against my task. I was ashamed of this *false* modesty... Ten years behind me when quite simply the *nourishment* of my spirit had been at a standstill, when I had learnt nothing more that was usable, when I had forgotten a ridiculous amount about a hotchpotch of fusty erudition. Crawling through ancient metricians with meticulous precision and bad eyes—things had got that bad with me!—With a look of pity I saw how utterly emaciated I was, how I had wasted away: *realities* were entirely lacking within my knowledge, and the 'idealities' were worth damn all!—I was gripped by a really burning thirst: from then on, indeed, I pursued nothing but physiology, medicine, and natural science—I returned even to truly historical studies only when my *task* compelled me imperiously to do so. That was also when I first guessed the connection between an activity chosen contrary to one's instinct, a so-called 'profession', to which one is called *last of all*,* and that need to have one's feeling of emptiness and hunger *anaesthetized* through narcotic art—for example through Wagnerian art. When I looked around me more carefully I discovered that a large number of young men face the same crisis: one perversity positively *compels* a second. In Germany, in the 'Reich', to be quite explicit, all too many are doomed to make up their minds inopportunely and then, beneath a burden they can no longer shed,

waste away... They demand Wagner like an *opiate*—they forget themselves, they lose themselves for a moment... What am I saying! for *five
or six hours!*—

4

At that stage my instinct decided implacably against yet more
giving way, going along with things, mistaking myself. Any kind
of life, the most unfavourable conditions, illness, poverty—anything
seemed to me preferable to that unworthy 'selflessness' which
I had entered into at first from ignorance, from *youth*, and in
which I later got bogged down from inertia, so-called 'feelings of
obligation'.—Now that *bad* inheritance from my father's side
came to my assistance in a way I cannot admire enough, and just
at the right time—basically a predestination to an early death.
Illness slowly released me: it saved me from making any break, from
taking any violent, offensive step. I lost no one's good-will at that
point, and indeed gained many people's. Likewise illness gave me
the right to completely overturn all my habits; it allowed me, *compelled* me to forget; it bestowed on me the gift of *having* to lie still,
remain idle, wait, and be patient... But that is what thinking is!...
All by themselves my eyes put an end to all bookwormery, otherwise known as philology: I was released from the 'book', and read
nothing more for years—the *greatest* favour I have ever done
myself!—That nethermost self, as if buried alive, as if made mute
beneath the constant *need* to pay heed to other selves (—which is
what reading is!) awoke slowly, shyly, hesitantly—but finally *it
spoke again*. I have never been so happy with myself as in my life's
periods of greatest illness and pain: you need only take a look at
Daybreak or *The Wanderer and His Shadow* to understand what
this 'return *to myself*' was: the highest kind of *recuperation!*... The
other kind simply followed on from this.—

5

Human, All Too Human, that monument to a rigorous self-discipline,
with which I swiftly dispatched all the 'higher swindle', 'idealism',

'fine feeling', and other femininities I had brought in, was written down in all essentials in Sorrento; it was finished off and given its final form during a winter in Basle under much less favourable circumstances than those in Sorrento. Basically it is Mr *Peter Gast*, at that time studying at Basle University and very devoted to me, who has the book on his conscience. I dictated, my head bandaged up and in pain; he copied out and made corrections, too—basically he was the actual writer, while I was just the author. When I finally got my hands on the finished book—to the great amazement of a seriously ill man—I sent two copies to Bayreuth among other places. By a miraculously meaningful coincidence a beautiful copy of the text of *Parsifal* reached me at the same time, with Wagner's dedication to me, 'his dear friend Friedrich Nietzsche, Richard Wagner, Church Councillor'.—This crossing of the two books— it seemed to me as if I heard them make an ominous sound. Did it not sound like the clash of *rapiers*?... At any rate that is how we both felt: for we both said nothing.—Around this time the first *Bayreuther Blätter* appeared: I realized *what* it had been high time for.—Incredible! Wagner had become pious...

6

How I was thinking about myself at that time (1876), with what immense assuredness I had my task and its world-historic aspects in hand, the whole book bears testimony to this, but in particular one very explicit passage:* except that here, too, with my instinctive cunning, I avoided using the little word 'I' and this time illuminated with world-historic glory not Schopenhauer or Wagner but one of my friends, the excellent Dr Paul Rée—fortunately much too refined an animal to... *Others* were less refined: I could always tell the hopeless cases among my readers, for instance the typical German professor, by the fact that on the basis of this passage they thought they had to understand the whole book as higher Réealism... In truth it contained the contradiction of five or six sentences of my friend's: for this, read the Preface to *On the Genealogy of Morals*.—The passage reads: 'but what is the main principle that has been arrived at by one of the boldest and coolest thinkers,

the author of the book *On the Origin of Moral Sensations* (*lisez:**
Nietzsche, the first *immoralist*), by means of his incisive and pene-
trating analyses of human behaviour? "The moral individual is
no closer to the intelligible world than to the physical one—*for*
there is no intelligible world..." This principle, hardened and
sharpened under the hammer blows of historical knowledge
(*lisez: revaluation of all values*), may perhaps at some future
point—1890!—serve as the axe which will be applied to the roots
of humanity's "metaphysical need"—whether more as a blessing
or a curse on humanity, who can say? But in any event as a principle
with the most significant consequences, at once fruitful and fearful,
and looking into the world with the *double vision* that all great
insights have'...

Daybreak

Thoughts on Morality as Prejudice*

I

With this book my campaign against *morality* begins. Not that it has the slightest whiff of gunpowder about it: provided you have some sensitivity in your nostrils you will smell something quite different and much sweeter about it. No big guns or even small ones: if the book's effect is negative, then its means are so much less so, these means from which the effect follows like a conclusion, *not* like a cannon shot.* The fact that you take your leave of the book shyly wary of everything that has hitherto been honoured and even worshipped under the name of morality is perfectly consistent with the fact that there is not a negative word to be found in the entire book, no attack, no malice—that instead it lies in the sun, plump, happy, like a sea creature sunning itself among rocks. Ultimately I was myself this sea creature: practically every sentence in the book was conceived, *hatched* in that riot of rocks near Genoa, where I was on my own and still had secrets to share with the sea. Even now, if I encounter the book by chance, practically every sentence becomes a tip with which I can pull up something incomparable from the depths once again: its whole hide quivers with the tender shudders of recollection. It excels at the not inconsiderable art of making things which dart by lightly and noiselessly, moments I call divine lizards, stay still a little—not, though, with the cruelty of that young Greek god who simply skewered the poor little lizard,* but nevertheless with something sharp, with my pen... 'There are so many dawns that have not yet broken'*—this *Indian* motto is inscribed on the door to this book. *Where* does its originator *seek* that new morning, that still undiscovered delicate blush with which another day—ah, a whole series, a whole world of new days!—sets in? In a *revaluation of all values*, in freeing himself from all moral values, in saying 'yes' to and placing trust in everything that has hitherto been forbidden, despised, condemned. This *yes-saying* book pours out its light, its love, its delicacy over nothing but bad things, it gives them back their 'soul', their good conscience, the lofty right and *prerogative* of existence. Morality is not attacked, it just no longer comes into consideration... This book closes with an 'Or?'—it is the only book to close with an 'Or?'...

2

My task, that of preparing the way for a moment of highest self-contemplation on humanity's part, a *great noon-day* when it will look back and look ahead, when it will step out from under the dominance of chance and the priests and for the first time ask the question 'why?' 'what for?' *as a whole*—this task follows necessarily from the insight that humanity has *not* found the right way by itself, that it is definitely *not* divinely ruled but that precisely among its holiest conceptions of value the instinct of negation, of corruption, the *décadence* instinct has seductively held sway. This is why the question of the origin of moral values is for me a question of the *utmost importance*, because it determines the future of humanity. The requirement to *believe* that everything is basically in the best hands and that one book, the Bible, gives conclusive reassurance about the divine direction and wisdom in the destiny of humanity is, if you translate it back to reality, the will to suppress the truth about the pitiful opposite, namely that humanity has so far been in the *worst* hands, that it has been ruled by those who turned out badly, the cunningly vindictive, the so-called 'saints', these world-slanderers and humanity-defilers. The crucial sign that the priest (—including those *hidden* priests, the philosophers) has become dominant not just within a particular religious community but overall, that *décadence* morality, the will to the end, passes for morality *as such*, is the absolute value bestowed on what is unegoistic and the hostility faced everywhere by what is egoistic. I consider anyone who does not agree with me on this point to be *infected*... But the whole world disagrees with me... Such a clash of values leaves a physiologist in no doubt whatsoever. Once the most minor organ in an organism so much

as begins to neglect to pursue its self-preservation, its energy
renewal, its 'egoism' with perfect assuredness, then the whole thing
degenerates. The physiologist demands that the degenerating part
be *excised*, he denies any solidarity with what is degenerating, he
is at the furthest remove from sympathizing with it. But the
degeneration of the whole, of humanity, is precisely what the
priest *wants*: this is why he *preserves* what is degenerating—this is
the price he pays for dominating it. What is the point of those
mendacious concepts, morality's *ancillary* concepts 'soul', 'spirit',
'free will', 'God', if not to bring about humanity's physiological
ruin?... If you distract from the seriousness of the self-preservation,
the energy increase of the body, *in other words of life*, if you
construct an ideal out of anaemia, 'the salvation of the soul' out
of contempt for the body, what else is that if not a *recipe* for
décadence?—Loss of weightiness, resistance to natural instincts,
in one word 'selflessness'—this is what has been called *morality*
till now... With *Daybreak* I first took up the struggle against the
morality of unselfing oneself. *—

The Gay Science
(*'la gaya scienza'*)*

Daybreak is a yes-saying book, profound but bright and generous. The same is true once again and to the highest degree of the *gaya scienza*: in almost every sentence here profundity and mischief go tenderly hand in hand. A verse which expresses gratitude for the most marvellous month of January I have ever experienced—the whole book is its gift—reveals only too well the depths from which 'science' has become *gay* here:

> You who with your flaming spear
> Splinter the ice in my soul,
> So that it now rushes headlong
> To the sea of its highest hope:
> Ever brighter, ever healthier,
> Free in the most loving necessity—
> Thus does it praise your miracles,
> Fairest Januarius!*

Who can have any doubts about what is meant here by 'highest hope' when they see the adamantine beauty of Zarathustra's first words shining out at the conclusion of the fourth book?*—Or when they read, at the end of the third book, the granite sentences with which a destiny *for all time* is first formulated?—The 'Songs of Prince Vogelfrei', for the most part composed in Sicily, quite explicitly call to mind the Provençal notion of 'gaya scienza', that unity of *singer*, *knight*, and *free-thinker* which distinguishes the marvellous early culture of the Provençal people from all ambiguous cultures; the very last poem in particular, 'To the Mistral', a boisterous dancing song which—if I may!—dances above and beyond morality, is a perfect Provençalism. —

Thus Spoke Zarathustra

A Book for Everyone and Nobody

I

Now I shall relate the story of *Zarathustra*. The basic conception of the work—the *thought of eternal recurrence*, this highest attainable formula of affirmation—belongs to the August of 1881: it was dashed off on a sheet of paper with the caption '6,000 feet beyond man and time'. On that day I was walking through the woods by Lake Silvaplana;* not far from Surlei I stopped next to a massive block of stone that towered up in the shape of a pyramid. Then this thought came to me.—If I think back a few months from this day, I find, as an omen, a sudden and profoundly decisive alteration in my taste, in music above all. *Zarathustra* as a whole may perhaps be counted as music—certainly a rebirth of the art of *listening* was a prerequisite for it. In a small mountain spa town not far from Vicenza, Recoaro, where I spent the spring of 1881, I discovered, together with my maestro and friend Peter Gast, likewise 'born again', that the phoenix of music flew past us with lighter and more radiant plumage than ever before. If, however, I think forwards from that day, as far as the sudden onset of delivery in the most improbable circumstances in February 1883—the final section, a few sentences of which I quoted in the Foreword, was completed at precisely the sacred hour when Richard Wagner died in Venice*—then the result is eighteen months for the pregnancy. This figure of exactly eighteen months ought to suggest, to Buddhists at least, that I am actually a female elephant.— The interval includes the '*gaya scienza*', which gives a hundred indications that something incomparable is near; latterly it gives the opening of *Zarathustra* itself,* and in the penultimate section of the fourth book* it gives Zarathustra's fundamental thought. This interval likewise includes the *Hymn to Life* (for mixed choir and orchestra), the score of which was published two years ago by E. W. Fritzsch in Leipzig: a perhaps not insignificant symptom of my condition that year, when the *affirmative* pathos par excellence, which I call the tragic pathos, dwelt in me to the highest degree. Some time in the future people will sing it in memory of me.—The text, to be quite explicit, since there is a misconception about it in circulation, is not by me: it is the astonishing inspiration of a young Russian woman with whom I was friendly at the time, Miss Lou von Salomé.* Anyone who can extract any sense at all from the final words of the poem will guess why I favoured and admired it: they have greatness about them. Pain is *not* seen as an objection to life: 'If you have no happiness left to give me, well then! *you still have your pain...*' Perhaps my music has greatness about it in this passage, too. (Last oboe note C sharp, not C natural. Printer's error.)—The following winter I lived not far from Genoa on the delightfully tranquil Bay of Rapallo, carved out between Chiavari and the foothills of Porto Fino. My health was not of the best; the winter cold and exceptionally rainy; a little *albergo*,* right by the sea, with the high sea at night making it impossible to sleep, offered in more or less all respects the opposite of what was desirable. Nevertheless, and almost as a proof of my principle that everything crucial occurs 'nevertheless', it was in this winter and these unfavourable circumstances that my *Zarathustra* was produced.—In the mornings I would head south, along the splendid road towards Zoagli, and climb up high past pine trees, overlooking the sea for miles; in the afternoon, as often as my health permitted, I walked around the whole bay from Santa Margherita over to Porto Fino. This place and this landscape have grown even further in my affection because of the great love which the unforgettable German Kaiser Friedrich III* felt for them; by chance I was on this coast again in the autumn of 1886, when he visited this little forgotten world of happiness for the last time.—On these two routes the whole first part of *Zarathustra* came to me, especially Zarathustra himself, as a type: or rather, he *ambushed me...*

2

To understand this type you first need to be clear about its physiological precondition, which is what I call *great health*.

I know of no better, no *more personal* way to explicate this concept than the way in which I already have done, in one of the final paragraphs of the fifth book of the '*gaya scienza*'. There it says: 'We who are new, nameless, hard to understand, we premature births of a yet unproven future, we require for a new end a new means, too, namely a new health, one that is stronger, craftier, tougher, bolder, merrier than all healths have been so far. Anyone whose soul thirsts to have experienced the entire compass of previous values and desiderata and to have circumnavigated the entire coastline of this "Mediterranean" of the ideal, anyone who wants to know from the adventures of his ownmost experience how it feels to be a conqueror and discoverer of the ideal, likewise to be an artist, a saint, a legislator, a sage, a scholar, a pious man, an old-style religious hermit: for this he is in need of one thing above all else, *great health*—of the kind you not only have but also still constantly acquire and have to acquire because time and again you give it up, have to give it up... And now that we have long been under way in this fashion, we Argonauts* of the ideal, more courageous perhaps than is sensible and often enough shipwrecked and damaged but, to repeat, healthier than we might be permitted to be, dangerously healthy, time and again healthy—it appears to us that, as a reward, we have an as yet undiscovered land ahead of us, whose borders no man has yet descried, a land beyond all previous lands and corners of the ideal, a world so over-rich in what is beautiful, alien, questionable, terrible, and divine that our curiosity as well as our thirst for possession are beside themselves—ah, henceforth we are insatiable!... How could we, after such prospects and with such a ravenous hunger in our knowledge and conscience, still be satisfied with *present-day man*? It is bad enough, but unavoidable, that we now observe his most worthy objectives and hopes with a seriousness that is difficult to maintain, and perhaps no longer even look... A different ideal runs on ahead of us, a wondrous, tempting ideal rich in dangers, which we would not want to persuade anyone to adopt, because we grant no one *the right to it* so easily: the ideal of a spirit who plays naively, in other words without deliberation and from an overflowing plenitude and powerfulness, with everything that has hitherto been called holy, good, untouchable, divine; for whom the highest thing which the people naturally enough take as their yardstick of value would mean something like danger, decay, abasement, or at least recuperation, blindness, temporary self-forgetting; the ideal of a human–over-human well-being and benevolence which will often enough appear *inhuman*, for instance when it sets itself up beside all previous earthly seriousness, beside all previous solemnity in gesture, word, tone, glance, morality, and task as the very incarnation of its unintentional parody—and with which, in spite of all that, perhaps *the great seriousness* at last begins, the true question-mark is at last set down, the destiny of the soul changes direction, the hand on the clock moves round, the tragedy *begins…*'*

3

—Does anyone, at the end of the nineteenth century, have a clear idea of what poets in strong ages called *inspiration*? If not, then I'll describe it.— With the slightest scrap of superstition in you, you would indeed scarcely be able to dismiss the sense of being just an incarnation, just a mouthpiece, just a medium for overpowering forces. The notion of revelation—in the sense that suddenly, with ineffable assuredness and subtlety, something becomes *visible*, audible, something that shakes you to the core and bowls you over—provides a simple description of the facts of the matter. You hear, you don't search; you take, you don't ask who is giving; like a flash of lightning a thought flares up, with necessity, with no hesitation as to its form—I never had any choice. A rapture whose immense tension is released from time to time in a flood of tears, when you cannot help your step running on one moment and slowing down the next; a perfect being-outside-yourself* with the most distinct consciousness of myriad subtle shudders and shivers right down to your toes; a depth of happiness where the most painful and sinister things act not as opposites but as determined, as induced, as a *necessary* colour within such a surfeit of light; an instinct for rhythmic conditions that spans wide spaces of forms—length, the need for a rhythm with a *wide span* is practically the measure of the power of the inspiration, a kind of compensation for its pressure and tension... Everything happens to the highest degree involuntarily, but as if in a rush of feeling free, of unconditionality, of power, of divinity... The involuntariness of images and analogies is the most remarkable thing; you lose your sense of what is an image, what an analogy; everything offers itself as the nearest, most correct, most straightforward expression. It really seems—to recall a phrase of Zarathustra's—as though the things themselves were stepping forward and offering themselves for allegorical purposes (—'here all things come caressingly to your discourse and flatter you: for they want to ride on your back. On every allegory you ride here to every truth. Here the words and word-shrines of all Being spring open for you; all Being wants to become word here, all Becoming wants to learn from you how to talk—'*). This is *my* experience of inspiration; I have no doubt that you need to go back millennia in order to find someone who can say to me 'it is mine, too'.—

4

Afterwards I lay ill for a few weeks in Genoa. This was followed by a melancholy spring in Rome, when I put up with life—it was not easy. Basically I was irritated beyond measure by this most unconducive place on earth for the poet of *Zarathustra*, which I had not chosen voluntarily; I tried to get away—I wanted to go to *Aquila*, the counter-concept to Rome, founded out of enmity towards Rome, as I shall one day found a place in memory of an atheist and enemy of the church *comme il faut*,* one who is most closely related to me, the great Hohenstaufen emperor Friedrich II.* But there was a fatality about all this: I had to come back again. In the end I contented myself with the Piazza Barberini, after my efforts to find an *anti-Christian* locality had tired me out. I am afraid that once, so as to avoid bad smells as much as possible, I even asked at the Palazzo del Quirinale* whether they might not have a quiet room for a philosopher.—On a *loggia* high above the said piazza, from which you look out over all Rome and hear the *fontana* playing far below, that loneliest ever song was composed, the 'Night-Song';* around this time I was always accompanied by a melody of ineffable melancholy, whose refrain I recognized in the

words 'dead from immortality...'. In the summer, returning home
to the sacred spot where the first lightning-bolt of the thought of
Zarathustra had flashed before me, I found the Second Part of
Zarathustra. Ten days were enough; in no case—whether with
the first or with the third and last part*—did I need more. The
following winter, beneath the halcyon sky of Nice, which shone
into my life for the first time at that stage, I found the Third Part
of *Zarathustra*—and was finished. Scarcely a year needed for the
whole. Many hidden spots and high-spots from the landscape of
Nice have been consecrated for me by unforgettable moments;
that crucial part which bears the title 'On Old and New Tablets'*
was composed during the most laborious ascent from the station
to the wonderful Moorish mountain lair of Eza—my muscular
agility has always been at its greatest when my creative energy is
flowing most abundantly. The *body* is inspired: let's leave the
'soul' out of it... I could often be seen dancing;* in those days
I could be walking around on mountains for seven or eight hours
without a trace of tiredness. I slept well and laughed a lot—I was
the epitome of sprightliness and patience.

5

Aside from these works of ten days the years during and, above all,
after Zarathustra were ones of unparalleled crisis. You pay dearly
for being immortal: it means you die numerous times over the
course of your life.—There is something I call the *rancune* * of the
great: everything great, be it a work or a deed, once it has been
accomplished, immediately turns *against* whoever did it. By virtue
of having done it, he is now *weak*—he can no longer endure his
deed, can no longer face up to it. To have something *behind* you that
you should never have wanted, something that constitutes a nodal
point in the destiny of humanity—and from then on to have it *on top
of* you!... It almost crushes you... The *rancune* of the great!—
Another thing is the terrible silence you hear around you. Solitude
has seven skins; nothing gets through any more. You come to people,
you greet friends: a new wilderness; no one greets you with their gaze
any more. At best a kind of revolt. I experienced such a revolt, to

very varying degrees but from almost everyone close to me; it seems that nothing causes more profound offence than suddenly letting a distance be remarked—the *noble* natures who do not know how to live without honouring are rare.—A third thing is the absurd sensitivity of the skin to little stings, a kind of helplessness in the face of every little thing. This seems to me to result from the immense squandering of all one's defensive energies which every *creative* deed, every deed that derives from one's ownmost, innermost depths has as its precondition. This means that the *little* defensive capacities are, in a manner of speaking, suspended; no energy flows to them any more.—I might yet venture to suggest that one's digestion is worse, one moves about unwillingly, one is all too exposed to frosty feelings and mistrust, too—which in many cases is merely an aetiological error. In such a state I once sensed the proximity of a herd of cows even before I saw it, prompted by the return of milder, more philanthropic thoughts: *they* have a warmth about them…

6

This work stands entirely on its own. Let us leave the poets aside: absolutely nothing has ever been achieved, perhaps, from a comparable surfeit of strength. My concept of 'Dionysian' became the *highest deed* here; measured against it, all the rest of human action appears poor and limited. The fact that a Goethe, a Shakespeare would not be able to breathe for a moment in this immense passion and height, that Dante, compared with Zarathustra, is just one of the faithful and not one who first *creates* the truth, a *world-governing* spirit, a destiny—that the poets of the Veda* are priests and not even worthy of unfastening a Zarathustra's shoe-latches, this is all the very least that can be said and it gives no conception of the distance, the *azure blue* solitude in which this work lives. Zarathustra has an eternal right to say: 'I draw circles around myself and sacred boundaries; fewer and fewer climb with me upon ever higher mountains—I build a mountain-range from ever more sacred mountains.'* If you roll into one the spirit and the goodness of all great souls, all of them together would not be capable of producing a single speech of Zarathustra's. Immense is the ladder on which he climbs up and down; he has seen further, willed further, *achieved* further than any man. He contradicts with every word, this most affirmative of all spirits; in him all opposites are fused together into a new unity. The highest and the lowest powers of human nature, that which is sweetest, airiest, and most fearsome pours forth from a single spring with immortal assuredness. Till that point people do not know what height and depth are; still less do they know what is truth.* There is not a moment in this revelation of truth that might already have been anticipated or guessed by one of the greatest. There is no wisdom, no soul-study,* no art of speaking before Zarathustra; what is nearest, most everyday speaks here of unprecedented things. Aphorisms quivering with passion; eloquence become music; lightning-bolts hurled on ahead towards hitherto unguessed-at futures. The mightiest power of analogy that has yet existed is feeble fooling compared to this return of language to its natural state of figurativeness.*—And how Zarathustra descends and says the kindest things to everyone! How he tackles even his adversaries, the priests, with delicate hands and suffers from them with them!—Here man is overcome at every moment; the concept of 'overman' has become the highest reality here—everything that has hitherto been called great about man lies at an infinite distance *below* him. The halcyon tone, the light feet, the omnipresence of malice and high spirits and everything else that is typical of the type Zarathustra has never been dreamed of as essential to greatness. Precisely in this extent of space, in this ability to access what is opposed, Zarathustra feels himself to be the *highest of all species of being*; and when we hear how he defines it, we will dispense with searching for his like.

—the soul that has the longest ladder and so reaches down deepest,

the most comprehensive soul, that can run and stray and roam the farthest within itself,

the most necessary soul, that with pleasure plunges itself into chance,

the being soul, that *wills* to enter Becoming; the having soul, that *wills* to enter willing and longing—

that flees from itself and retrieves itself in the widest circles,

the wisest soul, which folly exhorts most sweetly,

the soul that loves itself the most, in which all things have their streaming and counter-streaming and ebb and flood*— —

But that is the concept of Dionysus himself.— This is precisely the direction in which a further consideration also leads. The psychological problem about the type of Zarathustra is how one who to an unprecedented degree says 'no', *does* 'no' to everything people previously said 'yes' to, can nevertheless be the opposite of a no-saying spirit; how the spirit that bears the weightiest of destinies, a fatality of a task, can nevertheless be the lightest and most otherworldly—Zarathustra is a dancer—how one who has the harshest, most terrible insight into reality, who has thought the 'most abyssal thought', nevertheless finds in it no objection to existence, or even to the eternal recurrence of existence—but rather yet another reason *to be himself* the eternal 'yes' to all things, 'the enormous and unbounded Yea- and Amen-saying'*... 'Into all abysses I carry my blessing Yea-saying'*... *But that is the concept of Dionysus once again.*

7

—What language will such a spirit speak when it talks to itself alone? The language of the *dithyramb*. I am the inventor of the dithyramb. Just listen to how Zarathustra talks to himself 'Before the Sunrise': no tongue before me had such emerald happiness, such divine delicacy. Even the most profound melancholy of such a Dionysus is still turned into a dithyramb; I will take, as an indication, the 'Night-Song', his immortal lament at being condemned not to love by the superabundance of light and power, by his *sunlike* nature.

Night it is: now all springing fountains talk more loudly. And my soul too is a springing fountain.

Night it is: now all songs of lovers at last awaken. And my soul too is the song of a lover.

Something unstilled, unstillable is within me, that wants to become loud. A desire for love is within me, that itself talks in the language of love.

Light am I: ah, would that I were night! But this is my solitude, that I am girded round with light.

Ah, would that I were dark and night-like! How I would suckle at the breasts of light!

And you yourselves would I yet bless, you little twinkling stars and fireflies up above!—and be blissful from your light-bestowals.

But I live in my very own light, I drink back the flames that break out from within me.

I know none of the happiness of him who takes; and often have I dreamed that stealing must be more blessèd than taking.

This is my poverty, that my hand never rests from bestowing; this is my envy, that I see expectant eyes and illumined nights of yearning.

Oh the wretchedness of all who bestow! Oh the eclipse of my sun! Oh the desire for desiring! Oh the ravenous hunger in satiety!

They take from me: but do I yet touch their souls? A chasm there is between taking and giving; and the smallest chasm is the last to be bridged.

A hunger grows from my beauty: I should like to cause pain to those I illumine, should like to rob those upon whom I have bestowed—thus do I hunger after wickedness.

Withdrawing the hand when another hand reaches out for it; like the waterfall, which hesitates even in plunging—thus do I hunger after wickedness.

Such revenge my fullness devises, such spite wells up from my solitude.

My joy in bestowing died away through bestowing, my virtue grew weary of itself in its overflow!

He who always bestows is in danger of losing his sense of shame; he who always distributes has hands and heart calloused from sheer distributing.

My eye no longer brims over at the shame of those who beg; my hand has grown too hard for the trembling of hands that are filled.

Where has the tear gone from my eye and the soft down from my heart? Oh the solitude of all who bestow! Oh the reticence of all who shine forth!

Many suns circle in barren space: to all that is dark they speak with their light—to me they are silent.

Oh this is the enmity of light toward that which shines: mercilessly it pursues its courses.

Unjust in its inmost heart toward that which shines, cold toward suns—thus wanders every sun.

Like a storm the suns wander along their courses; their inexorable will they follow, that is their coldness.

Oh, it is only you, dark ones, and night-like, who create warmth from that which shines! Oh, it is only you who drink milk and comfort from the udders of light!

Ah, ice is around me, my hand is burned on what is icy! Ah, thirst is within me, and it languishes after your thirst.

Night it is: ah, that I must be light! And thirst for the night-like! And solitude!

Night it is: now like a spring my desire flows forth from me—I am desirous of speech.

Night it is: now all springing fountains talk more loudly. And my soul too is a springing fountain.

Night it is: now all songs of lovers awaken. And my soul too is the song of a lover.—*

8

Nothing like this has ever been composed, ever been felt, ever been *suffered*: this is how a god suffers, a Dionysus. The answer to such a dithyramb of solar solitude in the light would be Ariadne*... Who knows apart from me what Ariadne is!... To all such riddles no one has yet had the solution; I doubt anyone has ever even seen riddles here.—At one point Zarathustra strictly specifies his task—it is mine, too—so that no one can be mistaken about its *sense*: he is *yes-saying* to the point of justifying, of redeeming even all that is past.

I walk among human beings as among fragments of the future: that future which I envisage.

And this is all my composing and striving, that I compose into one and bring together what is fragment and riddle and cruel coincidence.

And how could I bear to be human if the human being were not also a composer-poet and riddle-guesser and the redeemer of coincidence?

To redeem that which has passed away and to re-create all 'It was' into a 'Thus I willed it!'—that alone should I call redemption.*

Elsewhere he specifies as strictly as possible what 'man' can be for him alone—*not* an object of love, let alone of pity—Zarathustra has even gained mastery over his *great disgust* at man:* man to him is a formless material, an ugly stone in need of a sculptor.

Willing-no-more and *valuing*-no-more and *creating*-no-more: oh, that such great weariness might remain ever far from me!

In understanding, too, I feel only my will's joy in begetting and becoming; and if there be innocence in my understanding, that is because *the will to beget* is in it.

Away from God and Gods this will has lured me: what would there be to create if Gods—existed?

But to the human being it drives me again and again, my fervent creating-will; thus is the hammer driven to the stone.

Ah, you humans, in the stone there sleeps an image, the image of images! Ah, that it must sleep in the hardest, ugliest stone!

Now my hammer rages fiercely against the prison. Fragments fly from the stone: what is that to me!

I want to perfect it, for a shadow came to me—of all things the stillest and lightest once came to me!

The beauty of the Overhuman came to me as a shadow: what are the Gods to me now!…*

I will emphasize one final point, prompted by the highlighted verse. For a *Dionysian* task the hardness of the hammer, the *pleasure even in destroying* are crucial preconditions. The imperative 'Become hard!',* the deepest conviction *that all creators are hard*, is the true badge of a Dionysian nature. —

Beyond Good and Evil
Prelude to a Philosophy of the Future

1

The task for the years that now followed was marked out as strictly as possible. Now that the yes-saying part of my task was solved, it was the turn of the no-saying, *no-doing* half: the revaluation of previous values itself, the great war—the conjuring up of a day of decision. Included here is the slow look around for related people, for those who from strength would lend me a hand *in destroying*. —From then on all my writings are fish-hooks: perhaps I am as good as anyone at fishing?... If nothing was *caught*, then I am not to blame. *There weren't any fish...*

2

This book (1886) is in all essentials a *critique of modernity*, not excluding the modern sciences, the modern arts, even modern politics, together with pointers towards an opposing type, as unmodern as possible, a noble, yes-saying type. In the latter sense the book is a *school for the gentilhomme*,* this concept understood more spiritually *and more radically* than ever before. You must have courage in your body to be able just to endure it, you mustn't have learnt to fear*... All the things the age is proud of are felt as contradictions of this type, almost as bad manners, for example the famous 'objectivity', the 'sympathy with all that suffers', the 'historical sense' with its toadying to foreign taste, its grovelling to *petits faits*,* the 'scientificity'.— If you consider that the book follows *after Zarathustra*, then perhaps you will also guess the dietary regime without which it could not have come into being. The eye, indulged by a tremendous compulsion to see into the *distance*—Zarathustra is even more far-sighted than the Tsar*— is forced here to focus on what is closest, the present, what is *around us*. In all aspects, and especially in its form, you will find the same *capricious* turning away from the instincts which made a Zarathustra possible. Refinement in form, in intention, in the art of *silence* is in the foreground; psychology is handled with avowed harshness and cruelty—the book is devoid of any good-natured word... All this aids recuperation: after all, who could guess just *what* a recuperation is called for by such a squandering of goodness as is Zarathustra?... Theologically speaking—and listen well, for I rarely speak as a theologian—it was God himself who lay down in the form of a serpent under the Tree of Knowledge when his days' work was done: that was his way of recuperating from being God... He had made everything too beautiful... The Devil is just God being idle on that seventh day*...

Genealogy of Morals*

A Polemic

The three essays that make up this genealogy are perhaps, as regards their expression, intention, and art of surprise, the uncanniest thing yet written. Dionysus, as is well known, is also the god of darkness. —Each time a beginning that is *intended* to lead astray, cool, scientific, even ironic, intentionally foreground, intentionally off-putting. Gradually more agitation; patches of sheet lightning; very unpleasant truths growing louder from afar with a muffled drone—till finally a *tempo feroce** is reached, when everything drives forward with immense excitement. At the end each time, among absolutely terrible detonations, a *new* truth visible between thick clouds.— The truth of the *first* essay is the psychology of Christianity: the birth of Christianity out of the spirit of resentment, *not*, as is commonly believed, out of the 'spirit'—essentially a counter-movement, the great revolt against the dominance of *noble* values. The *second* essay gives the psychology of *conscience*: this is *not*, as is commonly believed, 'the voice of God in man'— it is the instinct of cruelty turned back on itself when it can no longer discharge itself outwards. Cruelty brought to light here for the first time as one of the oldest and most entrenched of cultural foundations. The *third* essay gives the answer to the question of where the immense *power* of the ascetic ideal, the priestly ideal, springs from, even though it is the *harmful* ideal par excellence, a will to the end, a *décadence* ideal. Answer: *not* because God is at work behind the priests, as is commonly believed, but *faute de mieux*— because it was the only ideal till now, because it had no competition. 'For man will rather will nothingness than *not* will'*... Above all there was no *counter-ideal—till Zarathustra.*—I have been understood. Three decisive preliminary works of a psychologist towards a revaluation of all values.— This book contains the first psychology of the priest.

Twilight of the Idols

How to Philosophize with a Hammer

This work of not even 150 pages, cheerful and fateful in tone, a demon that laughs—the product of so few days that I hesitate to say how many—is the absolute exception among books: there is nothing richer in substance, more independent, more subversive—more wicked. Anyone who wants to get a quick idea of how topsy-turvy everything was before I came along should make a start with this work. What the title-page calls *idol* is quite simply what till now has been called 'truth'. *Twilight of the Idols*—in plain words: the old truth is coming to an end...

2

There is no reality, no 'ideality' that is not touched on in this work (—'touched on': what a cautious euphemism!...) Not just the *eternal* idols, but also the most recent of all, hence the most doddery. 'Modern ideas', for example. A great wind blows through the trees, and all around fruits drop down—truths. It has in it the profligacy of an all-too-rich autumn: you trip over truths, you even trample some to death—there are too many of them... But what you lay your hands on is nothing still doubtful, rather decisions. I am the first to have the yardstick for 'truths' in my hand, I am the first to *be able* to decide. As if a *second consciousness* had grown within me, as if 'the will' had lit a light within me to shine on the *wrong* path which it had been heading down so far... The *wrong* path—people called it the way to 'truth'... All 'dark stress' is over with; it was precisely the *good* man who had the least idea about the right way*... And in all seriousness, no one before me knew the right way, the way *upwards*: only after me are there hopes, tasks, paths to prescribe to culture once again—*I am their evangelist*... And that is why I am also a destiny. — —

3

Immediately after finishing the aforementioned work and without wasting so much as a day I set about the immense task of the *Revaluation*,* with a sovereign feeling of pride to which nothing else comes close, every moment sure of my immortality and engraving sign after sign in tablets of bronze with the certainty of a destiny. The preface was produced on 3 September 1888: that morning, after I had written it down, I stepped outside and found before me the most beautiful day the Upper Engadine has ever shown me—limpid, aglow with colour, containing within itself all opposites, all gradations between ice and south.—Not until 20 September did I leave Sils-Maria, detained by floods till in the end I was long since the only visitor in this wonderful place, on which my gratitude wants to bestow the gift of an immortal name. After a journey beset by incident, even life-threatening danger from the floods in Como, which I did not reach till deep into the night, I arrived on the afternoon of the 21st in Turin, my *proven* place, my residence from now on. I took the same apartment again as I had had in the spring, via Carlo Alberto 6, III, opposite the mighty Palazzo Carignano, where Vittore Emanuele was born, looking out onto the Piazza Carlo Alberto and the hills beyond. Without hesitating and without letting myself be distracted for a moment, I went to work again: just the last quarter of the work was still to be polished off. On 30 September a great triumph; completion of the *Revaluation*; a god at his leisure beside the Po. That same day, moreover, I wrote the *foreword* to *Twilight of the Idols*, correcting the proofs of which had been my relaxation in September.—I have never experienced such an autumn, never even thought such a thing possible on earth—a Claude Lorrain imagined into infinity, every day of the same unbridled perfection. —

The Wagner Case

A Musician's Problem

I

To do this work justice you need to be suffering from the fate of music as if from an open wound.—*What* do I suffer from when I suffer from the fate of music? The fact that music has been robbed of its world-transfiguring, yes-saying character—that it is *décadence* music and no longer the flute of Dionysus... But assuming that you feel for the cause of music in this way as if it were your *own* cause, the history of your *own* suffering, then you will find this work full of considerations and excessively mild. In such cases being cheerful and good-naturedly mocking oneself as well— *ridendo dicere severum*,* where *verum dicere** would justify any amount of harshness—is humaneness itself. Does anyone really doubt that, as an old artillerist, I am able to bring up my *big* guns against Wagner?—I kept to myself everything decisive in this matter—I loved Wagner.—Ultimately my task's purpose and path contains an attack on a more subtle 'unknown', not easily guessed by anyone else—oh, I have still to expose 'unknowns' quite different from a Cagliostro of music—still more, of course, an attack on the German nation, which in spiritual matters is becoming ever more sluggish and poorer in instinct, ever more *honest*, and which with an enviable appetite continues to nourish itself on opposites and gulps down 'faith' as well as scientificity, 'Christian charity' as well as anti-Semitism, the will to power (to the 'Reich') as well as the *évangile des humbles*,* without troubling its digestion... What impartiality between opposites! what gastric neutrality and 'selflessness'! What a sense of fairness the German *palate* has, giving everything equal rights—finding everything to its taste... Without a shadow of a doubt, the Germans are idealists... The last time I visited Germany I found German taste striving to grant equal rights to Wagner and the Trumpeter of Säckingen;* I myself witnessed *at first hand* the founding in Leipzig, in honour of Master

Heinrich Schütz—one of the most genuine and German of musicians, German in the old sense of the word, not just a Reich
German—of a Liszt Association, with the aim of preserving and
promoting *wily* church music*... Without a shadow of a doubt,
the Germans are idealists...

2

But at this point nothing will prevent me becoming coarse and
telling the Germans a few harsh truths: *who else will do it?*—I am
talking about their indecency *in historicis*.* Not only have German
historians entirely lost the *broad view* of the course, the values of
culture and are, to a man, buffoons of politics (or of the Church—):
this broad view is even *proscribed* by them. You must first be
'German', have a 'pedigree', then you can decide on all values
and non-values *in historicis*—you establish them... 'German' is
an argument, 'Deutschland, Deutschland über Alles'* a principle,
the Teutons are the 'ethical world order' in history; in comparison to the *imperium romanum** they are the bearers of freedom, in
comparison to the eighteenth century the restorers of morality, of
the 'categorical imperative'*... There is a Reich German kind of
historiography; there is, I fear, even an anti-Semitic kind—there
is a *court* historiography and Herr von Treitschke is not ashamed...
Recently an idiotic judgement *in historicis*, a statement by the
fortunately deceased aesthetically minded Swabian Vischer, did
the rounds of the German newspapers as a 'truth' with which every
German *would have to agree*: 'The Renaissance *and* the Reformation,
only the two together make a whole—the aesthetic rebirth *and*
the ethical rebirth.'—With such statements my patience runs out
and I feel the desire, even the duty to tell the Germans once and
for all just *what* they have on their consciences. *They have on their
consciences all the great cultural crimes of four centuries!*... And always
for the same reason, because of their innermost *cowardice* in the face
of reality, which is also a cowardice in the face of truth, because of
the untruthfulness that has become instinctual with them, because
of 'idealism'... The Germans robbed Europe of the harvest, the
meaning of the last *great* period, the Renaissance period, at the

point when a higher order of values, when the noble, life-affirming, future-confirming values had achieved a victory at the seat of the opposing values, the *values of decline—and had reached right into the instincts of those sitting there!* Luther, that disaster of a monk, restored the Church, and, what is a thousand times worse, Christianity, at the very point *when it was succumbing...* Christianity, this *denial of the will to life* made into a religion!... Luther, an impossible monk who, for reasons of his 'impossibility', attacked the Church and—consequently!—restored it... The Catholics would have good reason to celebrate Luther festivals, compose Luther plays... Luther—and 'ethical rebirth'! The devil take all psychology! Without a doubt, the Germans are idealists.—Just when an honest, unambiguous, perfectly scientific mentality had been achieved, through immense bravery and self-overcoming, the Germans were twice able to find ways to creep back to the old 'ideal', to reconcile truth and 'ideal', basically formulas for a right to reject science, for a right to *lie*. Leibniz and Kant—the two greatest impediments to Europe's intellectual honesty!—Finally, when a *force majeure* of genius and will came into view on the bridge between two centuries of *décadence*, strong enough to forge Europe into a unity, a political *and economic* unity, for the purpose of ruling the world, the Germans with their 'Wars of Liberation'* robbed Europe of the meaning, the miracle of meaning in the existence of Napoleon—so they have on their consciences everything that came about and exists today: nationalism, the *most anti-cultural* illness and unreason there is, the *névrose nationale** that ails Europe, the perpetuation of Europe's petty-statery, of *petty* politics: they have even robbed Europe of its meaning, its *reason*—they have led it up a blind alley.—Does anyone beside me know a *way* out of this blind alley?... A task great enough to *bind together* the nations again?...

3

—And in the end, why should I not put my suspicion into words? Even in my case the Germans will once again try everything to turn the labour of an immense destiny into the birth of a mouse.*

They have compromised themselves over me thus far, and I doubt they will do any better in future.—Ah, how I yearn to be a *bad* prophet in this respect!... At present my natural readers and listeners are Russian, Scandinavian, and French—will they always be so?—The Germans are inscribed in the history of knowledge with nothing but ambiguous names; they have only ever produced 'unconscious' counterfeiters (—Fichte, Schelling, Schopenhauer, Hegel, Schleiermacher deserve to be called this just as much as Kant and Leibniz; they are all just veil-makers*—): they shall never have the honour of seeing the first *honest* spirit in the history of spirit, the spirit in which the truth comes to pass judgement on four millennia of counterfeiting, conflated with the German spirit. The 'German spirit' is *my* bad air: I have difficulty breathing when near the uncleanliness *in psychologicis** become instinct which a German's every word, every expression betrays. They never went through a seventeenth century of harsh self-examination like the French; a La Rochefoucauld, a Descartes are a hundred times superior to the foremost Germans in honesty—to this day they have never had a psychologist. But psychology is practically the yardstick of a race's *cleanliness* or *uncleanliness*... And if you are not even cleanly, how can you be *profound*? A German is almost like a woman in that you can never get to the bottom of him: *he doesn't have one*, that is all. But that doesn't even make you shallow.* —What they call 'profound' in Germany is precisely this instinctual uncleanliness towards oneself which I am now talking about: people don't *want* to be clear about themselves. Should I not suggest the word 'German' as an international coinage for *this* psychological depravity?—At the moment, for example, the German Kaiser is calling it his 'Christian duty' to free the slaves in Africa: we *other* Europeans, then, would call that just 'German'... Have the Germans produced even one single book that was profound? They lack even the concept of what is profound in a book. I have known scholars who considered Kant profound; at the Prussian court, I fear, they consider Herr von Treitschke profound. And when I occasionally praise Stendhal as a profound psychologist, I have come across university professors who had me spell the name...

4

—And why should I not go right to the limit? I love clearing the decks. It is even a part of my ambition to be known as the despiser of the Germans par excellence. I expressed my *mistrust* of the German character when I was as young as 26 (third *Untimely*, p. 71)*—for me, the Germans are impossible. If I imagine a kind of man who runs counter to all my instincts, then the result is always a German. The first thing I check when testing a man's kidney is whether he has a feeling for distance in his body, whether he sees rank, degree, order between man and man everywhere, whether he *distinguishes*: that is what makes for a *gentilhomme*; anything else and you fall irredeemably under the charitable, oh so good-natured concept of *canaille*. But the Germans are *canaille*—oh! they are so good-natured... You demean yourself by associating with Germans: the German makes things equal... If I leave aside my association with a few artists, above all with Richard Wagner, then I have not spent a single pleasant hour with Germans... If the most profound spirit in all millennia were to appear among Germans, then some saviour of the Capitol* would fondly imagine that her highly un-beautiful soul* ought at least to be taken into consideration, too... I cannot stand this race with which one is always in bad company, which has no fingers for nuances—woe is me! I am a nuance—which has no *esprit* in its feet and cannot even walk... In the end the Germans have no feet at all, they just have legs... The Germans have no idea how vulgar they are, but that is the height of vulgarity—they are not even *ashamed* of being just Germans... They have a view on everything and even think their view decisive; I fear they have even decided about me... —My whole life is the strictest proof of these statements. In vain do I scan it for a sign of tactfulness, of *délicatesse** towards me. From Jews, yes, but never yet from Germans. It is in my nature to be mild-mannered and benevolent towards everyone—I have a *right* not to make any distinctions—this does not stop me keeping my eyes open. I make exception for no one, least of all my friends—in the end I hope that this has not detracted from my humaneness towards them! There are five or six things which have always been matters of

honour to me.—Nevertheless it remains the case that for years
I have felt almost every letter that has reached me to be an act of
cynicism: there is more cynicism in the benevolence I am shown
than in any amount of hatred... I tell each of my friends to their
face that they have never thought it worth the trouble *studying* any
of my writings; I can tell from the slightest signs that they don't
even know what's in them. And as for my *Zarathustra*, who of my
friends has seen in it anything more than an unwarranted and
thankfully entirely trivial presumption?... Ten years*—and no
one in Germany has had enough of a guilty conscience to defend
my name against the absurd silence under which it lay buried: it
was a foreigner, a Dane, who was the first to have enough subtlety
of instinct *and courage* to do so, and who was outraged by my supposed friends... At which university in Germany would it be possible nowadays to lecture on my philosophy as Dr Georg Brandes
did last spring in Copenhagen, thus proving himself to be even
more of a psychologist? I myself have never suffered from any of
this; what is *necessary* does me no harm; *amor fati** is my innermost nature. But this does not stop me from loving irony, even
world-historic irony. And so, roughly two years before the shat-
tering lightning-bolt of the *Revaluation*, which will have the earth
in convulsions, I sent *The Wagner Case* out into the world:* the
Germans should entirely fail to understand me once again and thus
immortalize themselves!* there's still time!—Has it happened?—
Exquisitely so, my dear Teutons! My compliments to you!... Not
forgetting my friends: an old friend has just written to me to say
that she now *laughs* at me... And this at a moment when I bear an
ineffable responsibility—when no word can be too tender, no look
reverent enough towards me. For I am carrying the destiny of
humanity on my shoulders.—

WHY I AM A DESTINY

I

I know my lot. Some day my name will be linked to the memory of something monstrous, of a crisis as yet unprecedented on earth, the most profound collision of consciences, a decision conjured up *against* everything hitherto believed, demanded, hallowed. I am not a man, I am dynamite.*—And for all that, there is nothing in me of a founder of religions—religions are for the rabble; I need to wash my hands after contact with religious people... I don't *want* any 'disciples'; I think I am too malicious to believe in myself; I never address crowds... I have a terrible fear of being declared *holy* one day: you can guess why I am publishing this book *beforehand*—it should prevent any mischief-making with me... I don't want to be a saint, and would rather be a buffoon... Perhaps I am a buffoon... And nevertheless—or rather *not* nevertheless, for till now there has never been anyone more hypocritical than saints—the truth speaks from me.—But my truth is *terrifying*, for *lies* were called truth so far.—*Revaluation of all values*: that is my formula for the highest act of self-reflection on the part of humanity, which has become flesh* and genius in me. My lot wills it that I must be the first *decent* human being, that I know I stand in opposition to the hypocrisy of millennia... I was the first to *discover* the truth, by being the first to sense—*smell*—the lie as a lie... My genius is in my nostrils... I contradict as no one has ever contradicted before and yet am the opposite of a no-saying spirit. I am an *evangelist* the like of which there has never been; I know tasks so lofty that there has not yet been a concept for them; I am the first to give rise to new hopes. Bearing all this in mind, I am necessarily also the man of impending disaster. For when the truth squares up to the lie of millennia, we will have upheavals, a spasm of earthquakes, a removal of mountain and valley* such as have never been dreamed of. The notion of politics will then completely dissolve into a spiritual war, and all configurations of power from the old society will be exploded—they are all based on a lie: there will be wars such as there have never yet been on earth. Only since I came on the scene has there been *great politics* on earth. —

2

Do you want a formula for a destiny like that, *which becomes man?** — You will find it in my *Zarathustra*.

> —*And whoever wants to be a creator in good and evil: verily, he must first be an annihilator and shatter values.*
> *Thus does the highest evil belong to the highest good: but this latter is the creative.**

I am by far the most terrifying human being there has ever been; this does not prevent me from being the most benevolent in future. I know the pleasure in *destroying* to an extent commensurate with my *power* to destroy—in both I obey my Dionysian nature, which is incapable of separating no-doing from yes-saying. I am the first *immoralist*: hence I am the *destroyer* par excellence. —

3

I have not been asked—I ought to have been asked—what precisely in my mouth, in the mouth of the first immoralist, the name *Zarathustra* means: for what makes that Persian incredibly unique in history is precisely the opposite of it. Zarathustra was the first to see in the struggle of good and evil the true driving-wheel in the machinery of things—the translation of morality into the metaphysical, as strength, cause, goal in itself, is *his* doing. But in principle this question would already be the answer. Zarathustra *created* the disastrous error that is morality: thus he must also be the first to *acknowledge* the mistake. It is not just that he has had longer and more experience of this than any other thinker—after all, the whole of history is the experimental refutation of the principle of the so-called 'moral world order'—more importantly, Zarathustra is more truthful than any other thinker. His teaching and it alone has as its highest virtue truthfulness—in other words the opposite of the *cowardice* of the 'idealist', who takes flight from reality; Zarathustra has more bravery in his body than all the other thinkers put together. Tell the truth and *shoot arrows well*, that is Persian virtue.*—Am I understood?... The self-overcoming of morality out of truthfulness, the self-overcoming of the moralist into his opposite—*me*—this is what the name of Zarathustra means in my mouth.

4

At root my term '*immoralist*' incorporates two denials. On the one hand I am denying a type of human being who has hitherto been considered the highest type—the *good*, the *benevolent*, the *beneficent*; on the other hand I am denying a kind of morality that has achieved validity and predominance as morality in itself—*décadence* morality, or to put it more concretely, *Christian* morality. The second contradiction could be seen as the more decisive, since, broadly speaking, the overestimation of goodness and benevolence strikes me as already a consequence of *décadence*, as a symptom of weakness, as irreconcilable with an ascendant and yes-saying life: denying *and destroying* are the preconditions for yes-saying.—Let me stay for a moment with the psychology of the good man. In order to judge what a type of human being is worth, you have to calculate how much it costs to maintain it—you have to know its conditions of existence. The condition of existence of the good is *lying*—put differently, not *wanting* at any price to see how reality is constituted, which is *not* in a manner so as to challenge benevolent instincts at every turn, still less so as to permit the intrusion of short-sighted, good-natured hands at every turn. Considering *emergencies* of every kind as an objection, as something to be *abolished*, is *niaiserie** par excellence, broadly speaking, a real disaster in its consequences, a destiny of stupidity—practically as stupid as the will to abolish bad weather—out of sympathy with the poor, perhaps... In the great economy of the whole the awfulness of reality (in the affects, in the desires, in the will to power) is incalculably more necessary than is that form of petty happiness, so-called 'goodness'; indeed you have to be indulgent to even give it house-room, such is its instinctual hypocrisy. I shall have a great opportunity to demonstrate for the whole of history the exceptionally uncanny consequences of *optimism*, this monstrous product of the *homines optimi*.* Zarathustra, the first to understand that the optimist is just as much a *décadent* as the pessimist and possibly more noxious, says: *good men never tell the truth. False coasts and securities the good have taught you; in the lies of the good you were born and bred. Everything has been lied about and twisted around down to its ground by the good*.* Fortunately the world is not constructed for the benefit of instincts, so that merely good-natured herd animals find their circumscribed happiness in it; demanding that everything should become 'good man', herd animal, blue-eyed, benevolent, 'beautiful soul'—or, as Mr Herbert Spencer would have it, altruistic—would mean depriving existence of its *great* character, castrating humanity and reducing it to a wretched chinoiserie.—*And this has been attempted!*... *This is precisely what people have called morality*... It is in this sense that Zarathustra calls the good at times 'the last men', at times the 'beginning of the end'; above all he senses they are *the most harmful kind of human being*, because they ply their existence both at the expense of the *truth* and at the expense of the *future*.

The good—they cannot *create*: they are always the beginning of the end—
—they crucify him who writes *new* values on new tablets, they sacrifice the future *to themselves*, they crucify all human future!
The good—they have always been the beginning of the end...
And whatever harm the world-slanderers may do, *the harm done by the good is the most harmful harm*.*

5

Zarathustra, the first psychologist of the good, is—consequently— a friend of the evil. When a *décadence* kind of man rises to the rank of the highest kind, this could only happen at the expense of the opposite kind, the strong man assured in life. When the herd animal beams in the gleam of the purest virtue, the exceptional man must have been devalued to become evil. When hypocrisy at any price lays claim to the perspective of 'truth', the really truthful man must go by the worst of names. Zarathustra leaves no room for doubt here: he says that it was precisely knowing the good people, the 'best' people, that made him shudder before humanity as a whole; it was *this* revulsion that gave him the wings 'on which to soar into distant futures'*—he makes no secret of the fact that *his* type of man, a relatively superhuman type, is superhuman precisely in relation to the *good*, that the good and the just would call his over-man a *devil*...

> You highest humans that my eye has encountered! This is my doubt concerning you, and my secret laughter: I suspect that you would call my Overhuman—Devil!
> So foreign are your souls to what is great, that the Overhuman would *terrify* you with his goodness...

It is here and nowhere else that one must make a start in order to understand what Zarathustra *wants*: the kind of man that he conceives, conceives reality *as it is*: it is strong enough for that—it is not alienated from it, not at one remove from it, it is *reality itself*, it has all its terrible and questionable aspects, too; *that is the only way man can have greatness*...

6

—But there is another reason, too, why I have chosen the word '*immoralist*' as my emblem, my badge of honour: I am proud to have this word that sets me apart from the whole of humanity. No one has yet felt *Christian* morality to be *beneath* them: for that you need an elevation, a far-sightedness, a hitherto quite unprecedented psychological depth and bottomlessness. Christian morality has hitherto been the Circe of all thinkers—they were in its service. —Who before me has climbed into the caves from which the poisonous fug of this kind of ideal—*world-denial!*—emanates? Who has dared even to suppose that they *are* caves? Who was there among philosophers before me who was a *psychologist* and not rather the opposite, a 'higher swindler', an 'idealist'? There just was no psychology before me.—Being the first here can be a curse, at any rate it is a destiny: *for you are also the first to despise*... *Disgust* at man is my danger*...

7

Have I been understood?—What sets me apart and aside from all the rest of humanity is having *discovered* Christian morality. This is why I was in need of a word that has the sense of a challenge to everyone. Not to have opened one's eyes here earlier strikes me as the greatest uncleanliness that humanity has on its conscience, as self-deception become instinct, as a fundamental will *not* to see everything that happens, every causality, every reality, as counterfeiting *in psychologicis* to the point of criminality. Blindness in the face of Christianity is the *crime* par excellence—the crime *against life*... The millennia, the nations, the first and the last, the philosophers and the old women—with the exception of five or six moments in history, with myself as a seventh—on this point they are all worthy of one-another. Hitherto the Christian was *the* 'moral being', an unparalleled curiosity—and *as* a 'moral being' more absurd, hypocritical, vain, thoughtless, *detrimental to himself* than the greatest despiser of humanity could ever dream of being. Christian morality—the most malignant form of the will to falsehood, the true Circe of humanity: the thing that *ruined* it. It is *not* the mistake as such that incenses me about this sight, *not* the millennia-old lack of 'good will', of discipline, of decency, of bravery in spiritual matters that its victory betrays—it is the lack of nature, it is the utterly dreadful fact that *anti-nature** itself has been receiving the highest honours as morality and as law, as categorical imperative,* has been hanging above humanity!... To misunderstand oneself so badly, *not* as an individual, *not* as a people, but as humanity!... The fact that people taught how to despise the primordial instincts of life, that people lyingly *invented* a 'soul', a 'spirit' so as to make the body shameful, the fact that people teach how to feel there is something impure about the prerequisite for life, sexuality, that people look for the principle of evil in that which is most profoundly necessary to flourishing, *strict* self-discipline (—the very word is slanderous!—), that, conversely, people see in the typical emblem of decline and instinctual contradictoriness, in the 'selfless', in the loss of weightiness, in 'depersonalization' and 'brotherly love' (—brotherly *dependency*!) *higher* value, what I am saying! *value in itself*!… What? Might humanity itself be in *décadence*? has it always been?—What is incontrovertible is that it has been *taught* only *décadence* values as the highest values. The morality of unselfing oneself is the morality of decline par excellence, the fact that 'I am being destroyed' translated into the imperative: 'you *should* all be destroyed'—and *not only* into the imperative!… The sole morality that has hitherto been taught, the morality of unselfing oneself, betrays a will to the end; at the most fundamental level it *denies* life. —Here the possibility might remain open that it is not humanity that is degenerating, but only that parasitic kind of man, the *priest*, who through morality has lied his way up to being the determiner of humanity's values—who realized that Christian morality was his means to *power*… And indeed this is *my* insight: the teachers, the leaders of humanity, theologians to a man, were also all *décadents*: *hence* the revaluation of all values into that which is hostile to life;* *hence* morality… *Definition of morality*: morality—the idiosyncrasy* of *décadents*, with the ulterior motive of avenging themselves *on life—and* succeeding. I set store by *this* definition. —

8

—Have I been understood?—I have not said a word just now that I might not have said five years ago through the mouth of Zarathustra. The *discovery* of Christian morality is an event without parallel, a real catastrophe. Anyone who raises awareness about it is a *force majeure*, a destiny—he breaks the history of humanity in two. You live *before* him or you live *after* him… The lightning-bolt of truth has struck precisely what stood highest hitherto: anyone who understands *what* has been destroyed there should look to see if he has anything left in his hands. Everything called 'truth' so far has been recognized as the most harmful, malicious, subterranean form of lie; the holy pretext of 'improving' humanity recognized as a ruse to *drain dry* life itself and make it anaemic. Morality as *vampirism**... Anyone who discovers morality discovers at the same time the valuelessness of all the values that are or have been believed in; in the most revered types of man, even those pronounced *holy*, he no longer sees anything venerable, but sees in them the most disastrous kind of deformity, disastrous *because fascinating*... The concept 'God' invented as a counter-concept to life—bringing together into one dreadful unity everything harmful, poisonous, slanderous, the whole mortal enmity against life! The concept 'hereafter', 'true world' invented in order to devalue the *only* world there is—so as to leave no goal, no reason, no task for our earthly reality! The concepts 'soul', 'spirit', ultimately even 'immortal soul' invented so as to despise the body, to make it sick—'holy'—so as to approach with terrible negligence all the things in life that deserve to be taken seriously, questions of food, accommodation, spiritual diet, the treatment of the sick, cleanliness, weather! Instead of health the 'salvation of the soul'—in other words a *folie circulaire** between penitential cramps and redemption hysteria! The concept 'sin' invented along with its accompanying torture instrument, the concept 'free will', so as to confuse the instincts and make mistrust of the instincts into second nature! In the concept of the 'selfless', the 'self-denying', the true emblem of *décadence* that turns being *enticed* by what is harmful, no longer being *able* to find what is in one's interest, self-destruction, into the badge of value itself, into 'duty', 'holiness', 'divinity' in man! Ultimately—and this is the most terrible thing—in the concept of the *good* man siding with everything weak, sick, misshapen, suffering from itself, everything *that ought to perish*—the law of *selection* crossed, an ideal made out of the contradiction to the proud man who turned out well, to the yes-saying, future-assured, future-confirming man—who is called *evil* from now on... And all this was believed in *as morality*!—*Écrasez l'infâme!**— —

9

—Have I been understood?—*Dionysus against the crucified one...*

EXPLANATORY NOTES

Ecce Homo: 'Behold the Man'. A self-application of Pontius Pilate's words as he reveals Jesus to the mob in the Vulgate (Latin) version of John 19: 5, previously used by Nietzsche as the title for the penultimate poem (62) in the collection 'Joke, Cunning, and Revenge', which forms the 'Prelude in German Rhymes' to *The Gay Science* (1882). The deliberate blasphemy of this title underlines the anti-Christian message of the book from the outset.

How To Become What You Are: reworking of the injunction *genoi hoios essi* ('become who you have learnt to be') in the Second Pythian Ode by the Greek poet Pindar (522–443 BC), first cited by Nietzsche in a letter to his friend Erwin Rohde over twenty years before (KSB 2: 235) and already reworked at GS 270.

FOREWORD

3 *'bear witness' to myself*: further allusion to the Gospel of St John, where this is a frequent motif (cf. e.g. John 5: 36–7; 8: 18; 10: 25; 15: 27; 18: 37).

Upper Engadine: valley in south-eastern Switzerland where Nietzsche spent most of his summers between 1879 and 1888. Contains Sils-Maria and St Moritz.

Dionysus: Greek god, first discussed in detail by Nietzsche in *The Birth of Tragedy* (1872) as the opposing 'artistic force of nature' to Apollo. In the later works he increasingly asserts an allegiance to Dionysus alone, and the operative contrast he emphasizes is with the Christian God; in *Ecce Homo* this culminates in the assertion of an identification in the final words of the book (IV 9). In a contemporary notebook, Nietzsche uses 'Dionysos philosophos'—the ideal of a (pagan) philosopher god—as a putative book title (KSA 13: 613).

Perhaps I have managed . . . the fake world and reality: brief recapitulation of four themes from Nietzsche's previous work, *Twilight of the Idols* (1888): a cheerfulness of tone, a critique of 'The "Improvers" of Humanity' (TI VII), the critique of 'idols' (*passim*), and a critique of the dualistic distinction between 'real' and 'apparent' worlds (TI IV).

4 *spirit*: 'Geist'. This translation has generally been preferred over 'mind' or 'intellect', although the German word means all three.

sincerity: 'Sauberkeit', the primary meaning of which is 'cleanliness'. Cf. I 8: 'I have an instinct for cleanliness that is utterly uncanny in its sensitivity.'

Nitimur in vetitum: 'We strive for what is forbidden', a quotation from the Roman poet Ovid (Publius Ovidius Naso, 43 BC–AD 18), *Amores*, III. iv. 17.

4 *will to power*: first mention in this text of a crucial term in Nietzsche's philosophy of the 1880s, his ultimate formulation of the 'Dionysian truth' of the world as a seething turmoil of appropriative, life-affirming, mutually opposing forces 'beyond good and evil' (cf. BGE 259; GM II 12). There are three other uses in *Ecce Homo*, at III 'BT' 4, III 'WC' 1, and IV 4.

5 *'It is the stillest words . . . direct the world—'*: slightly repunctuated quotation from Z II, 'The Stillest Hour'.

The figs . . . afternoon—: slightly repunctuated quotation from the opening of Z II, 'Upon the Isles of the Blest'. Also an allusion to Mark 11: 12–14, where the hungry Jesus curses a fig tree not yet in fruit.

décadent: key term in Nietzsche's late works, adopted from Paul Bourget. Nietzsche almost invariably uses the French word.

Alone I go now . . . alone!: based on John 13: 36 and 16: 32, where Jesus predicts his forthcoming death and abandonment by his disciples.

a statue fall and kill you!: cf. Aristotle, *Poetics*, IX, a classic example of 'poetic justice': 'We may cite the statue of Mitys at Argos, which fell upon his murderer while he was a spectator at a festival, and killed him' (1452a, 7–10).

when you have all denied me: allusion to Jesus's prediction of his denial by Peter, reported in all the gospels (Matthew 26: 34; Mark 14: 30; Luke 22: 34; John 13: 38).

Alone I go now . . . return to you . . .: slightly modified quotation from the end of the first part of *Thus Spoke Zarathustra* (1883–5: Z I, 'On the Bestowing virtue', 3).

6 *buried my forty-fourth year today*: the phrase (not a common one) indicates that the text was begun on Nietzsche's birthday, 15 October 1888, as a kind of birthday present to himself. In the draft version this paragraph was indeed dated.

'Revaluation of All Values': the title Nietzsche was still giving to the work he had just completed, *The Antichrist* (1888).

WHY I AM SO WISE

7 *fatefulness*: 'Verhängniss', one of a number of similar fate-related terms which Nietzsche uses in the course of the book. The commonest is 'Schicksal' ('destiny': cf. IV); others include 'Fatum' ('fate': I 6), 'Fatalismus' ('fatalism': I 6, III 'HA' 2), and 'Fatalität' ('fatality': I 7), 'verurtheilt' ('doomed': II 1, III 'HA' 3), and 'Loos' ('lot': IV 1). Cf. also the key term *'amor fati'* (II 10).

at the age of 36: i.e. in 1849, when Nietzsche was just 4 years old.

Naumburg: town in East Central Germany on the River Saale, where Nietzsche's mother lived from 1850 till her death in 1897. Nietzsche spent much of his childhood there and returned frequently over the rest of his active life to visit his mother and sister; after his collapse he lived there again from 1890 to 1897.

8 *the case of Socrates*: thematized in the second chapter of Nietzsche's previous work, *Twilight of the Idols*.

I have my hand in now, I am handy: 'Ich habe es jetzt in der Hand, ich habe die Hand dafür.' Punning start to the thematization of the hand and its associated metaphors of gripping, grasping, and understanding, which frequently recur over the course of the book (see especially III 'UM' 3).

9 *summa summarum*: Lat. 'sum of sums', i.e. (in this context) 'overall totality'.

when I stopped being a pessimist: i.e. when he renounced his allegiance to Schopenhauer's philosophy, in the late 1870s.

turned out well!: a paraphrase of the term 'Wohlgerathenheit' (cf. III 1), which is most often applied to children but is also a close translation of the ancient Greek concept of virtue as *arete*.

what does not kill him makes him stronger: cf. TI I 8: 'Whatever does not kill me makes me stronger.'

10 *Altenburg court*: Altenburg is a town in East Central Germany, capital of the Saxon duchy of Saxe-Altenburg, 1826–1918.

pur sang: Fr. 'of pure blood'. It was a family legend (since disproved) that the Nietzsche family was of Polish extraction. In the course of the 1880s Nietzsche himself increasingly came to espouse the idea, as a way of distancing himself from his German heritage.

canaille: Fr. 'riff-raff'.

disharmonia praestabilita: Lat. 'pre-established disharmony'. Ironic allusion to the doctrine of 'pre-established harmony' proposed by the German philosopher Leibniz to explain the interaction of mind and matter.

'eternal recurrence': first mention in this text of another of Nietzsche's central ideas from the 1880s, first formulated in *Thus Spoke Zarathustra* (cf. Z III, 'The Convalescent') and glossed later in *Ecce Homo* as 'the unconditional and infinitely repeated circulation of all things' (III 'BT' 3). There are three other uses in *Ecce Homo*, at III 'BT' 3, III 'Z' 1, and III 'Z' 6; in all cases the German term used is 'ewige Wiederkunft', although elsewhere Nietzsche occasionally also substitutes the term 'ewige Wiederkehr' ('eternal return').

the young German Kaiser: Wilhelm II, who had succeeded his father Friedrich III as German emperor and king of Prussia in June 1888, at the age of 29.

The rest is silence: Hamlet's last words from Act V, Scene 2 of Shakespeare's play, one of Nietzsche's favourite quotations.

The Pope: Leo XIII (reigned 1878–1903).

The higher natures . . . for the longest time: this motif of accumulation is developed at greater length in TI IX 44.

11 *a Dionysus head*: the reference here is obscure. The whole paragraph, with its ringing condemnation of Nietzsche's mother and sister on account of

the 'vulgarity' of their instincts, was suppressed by the latter and only restored to its rightful place in 1969 by Mazzino Montinari, co-editor of the standard German edition of Nietzsche's works. For the full details of this notorious episode, see Montinari's essay 'A New Section in Nietzsche's *Ecce Homo*', in his *Reading Nietzsche*, trans. Greg Whitlock (Urbana: University of Illinois Press, 2003), 103–40. The paragraph substituted by Elisabeth Förster-Nietzsche is now accepted as having been a superseded draft, but it was included in all editions of the text between 1908 and 1969, and ran as follows:

This double series of experiences, this ability to gain access to ostensibly separate worlds is reproduced in my nature in every respect—I am a doppelgänger, I have 'second' sight in addition to the first. *And* perhaps third sight, too . . . Even my extraction is enough to permit me a view beyond all merely local, merely nationally determined perspectives; it costs me no effort to be a 'good European'. On the other hand I am perhaps more German than present-day Germans, mere Reich Germans, could ever be—I, the last *antipolitical* German. And yet my ancestors were Polish nobility: it is from them that I have many racial instincts in my body—who knows? ultimately even the *liberum veto*. If I think of how often I am addressed as a Pole when I am travelling, and by Poles themselves, but how rarely I am taken for a German, then I might appear to be one of those whose Germanness is just *sprinkled on*. But my mother, Franziska Oehler, is at any rate something very German; likewise my paternal grandmother, Erdmuthe Krause. The latter spent the whole of her youth in the midst of good old Weimar, not without connections to Goethe's circle. Her brother, the Krause who was professor of theology in Königsberg, was appointed general superintendent in Weimar after Herder's death. It is not impossible that her mother, my great-grandmother, appears in the young Goethe's diary under the name 'Muthgen'. Her second marriage was to Superintendent Nietzsche in Eilenburg; on 10 October of the great war year 1813—the day Napoleon and his general staff entered Eilenburg—she gave birth. As a Saxon she was a great admirer of Napoleon; it may be that I still am, too. My father, born in 1813, died in 1849. Before he took over as minister to the parish of Röcken, near Lützen, he spent a few years living in Altenburg Castle, as teacher to the four princesses there. His pupils are the queen of Hanover, the Grand Duchess Constantine, the Grand Duchess of Oldenburg, and Princess Therese of Saxe-Altenburg. He was full of profound reverence towards the Prussian king Friedrich Wilhelm IV, from whom he also received his ministry; the events of 1848 were extremely distressing to him. I myself, born on the birthday of the said king, 15 October, was given the Hohenzollern names *Friedrich* Wilhelm, appropriately enough. There was one advantage, at least, to the choice of this day: throughout my childhood my birthday was a public holiday.—I consider it a great privilege to have had such a father: it even seems to me to explain all my other privileges—*not* including life, the great 'yes' to life. Above all it explains how no deliberate intention is required of me, but merely waiting, in order to enter involuntarily into a world of elevated and delicate things: I am at home there, only there is my innermost passion set free. The fact that I almost paid for this privilege with my life is certainly not an unfair deal.—To understand anything at all of my *Zarathustra* one needs perhaps to have the same qualification as I have—with one foot *beyond* life...

The *'liberum veto'* was the right of an individual deputy to the Polish parliament to dissolve a session and nullify all its legislation; 'the events of 1848' describes the series of uprisings across Europe in that year, which sought to establish more liberal governments.

that one instance: the ill-treatment he supposedly received from his mother and sister, as described in the previous paragraph.

grammar school in Basle: from his appointment to the chair of classical philology at Basle University in 1869 till he was granted a year's sick leave in 1876, Nietzsche was also obliged to teach at the local grammar school.

Sils-Maria: village in the Upper Engadine where Nietzsche spent his summers in 1881 and 1883–8.

Bayreuth: town in northern Bavaria, metonym (in Nietzsche's writings, at least) for the composer Richard Wagner, who lived there from 1872 till his death in 1883. Still the headquarters of the Wagner cult, and site of the 'Festspielhaus' where Wagner inaugurated a summer festival of his music in 1876.

12 *'brotherly love'*: 'Nächstenliebe', a first Christian concept to come under attack. Cf. II 3, II 9, IV 7, and Z I, 'On Love of One's Neighbour'.

'The Temptation of Zarathustra': planned title for Part Four of *Thus Spoke Zarathustra*, which Nietzsche was intending to republish in a much larger edition than the private edition of 1885. The incident referred to here occurs in Z IV, 'The Cry of Need'; and is a clear parody of the Temptation of Jesus (Matthew 4: 1–11; Mark 1: 12–13; Luke 4: 1–13).

13 *If a god came to earth . . . that would be divine*: taking up the theme of guilt and punishment from *On the Genealogy of Morals* (1887: GM II), in an explicitly anti-Christian context.

resentment: 'Ressentiment', a central concept first elaborated in *On the Genealogy of Morals* (GM I 10). The standard English translation, '*ressentiment*', characterizes it as a loan-word from the French, but Nietzsche spells it with an initial capital, stressing that he considers it to have been successfully adopted into the German language (which gives all nouns initial capitals)—by contrast with '*décadence*', for instance.

14 *'enmity comes to an end through friendship'*: cf. the first chapter of *The Dhammapada*, a collection of sayings attributed to the Buddha: 'Hatred does not cease by hatred, but only by love; this is the eternal rule.' On the Buddha as psychologist, see also AC 20.

15 *war*: this martial tone is typical of Nietzsche's late works and an aspect of his admiration for the Greek philosopher Heraclitus, who advocated that

war was 'the father of all things'. Cf. III 'UM', IV 1, and the foreword to *Twilight of the Idols* ('This little work is a *great declaration of war*').

15 *pathos*: here, as elsewhere, Nietzsche uses the term in its original Greek sense of 'passionate emotion' (by contrast with *ethos*, 'character').

Woman . . . is vengeful: first, relatively casual, instance of the repeated misogyny which mar(k)s the text. Cf. especially II 7, III 3, III 5, and III 'Z' 8.

David Strauss: object of Nietzsche's polemic in the first of his *Untimely Meditations, David Strauss, the Confessor and the Writer* (1873), specifically his book *Der alte und der neue Glaube: Ein Bekenntnis* (*The Old Faith and the New: A Confession*, 1872).

attacked Wagner: in *The Wagner Case* (1888) in particular.

16 *de rigueur*: Fr., here 'strict'.

self-overcoming: key term in Nietzsche's philosophy. Cf. III 'WC' 2, IV 3, and Z II, 'On Self-Overcoming': 'And this secret did Life herself tell to me. "Behold," she said, "I am *that which must always overcome itself.*"'

if I have been understood: first mention of a theme (and an anxiety) which will come to dominate the fourth chapter.

17 *pure folly*: ironic allusion to Wagner's last work, the 'stage-consecrating festival play' *Parsifal* (1882), whose hero is described as a 'pure [i.e. morally untainted] fool'. Nietzsche recycles this gibe several times in the text (cf. III 1, III 4).

adamantine: cf. the exchange between the diamond and the kitchen-coal in Z III, 'On Old and New Tablets', 29, used again as the conclusion to *Twilight of the Idols*.

18 *Yet what happened to me? . . . spitting into the wind*: slightly modified quotation from Z II, 'On the Rabble'.

WHY I AM SO CLEVER

19 *even as a child*: this is a blatant falsehood, considering that Nietzsche was brought up a perfectly orthodox Lutheran and confirmed at Easter 1861.

you shall not think: parody of the Ten Commandments (Exodus 20: 1–17).

virtù in the Renaissance style: Renaissance Italian stresses the etymological origin of the concept as 'manliness'.

moraline-free virtue: neologism which turns morality into a kind of chemical substance.

German education: a preoccupation of Nietzsche's ever since his early series of lectures 'On the Future of Our Educational Institutions' (1872). Cf. III 'UM' 1.

20 *Schopenhauer . . . 'will to life'*: Nietzsche chanced upon Schopenhauer's *magnum opus, Die Welt als Wille und Vorstellung* (*The World as Will and Representation*, 1819/44) in a second-hand bookshop in Leipzig in 1865

and was immediately enraptured. Here Schopenhauer advocates the 'self-suppression of the will', and argues that Christ should be interpreted as 'the symbol or personification of the denial of the will to live' (I 4, 70).

1866 was a turning point in this regard—: ironic reference to the short Austro-Prussian War of that year, which saw Prussia emerge victorious and establish hegemony among the German-speaking lands.

'alla tedesca': It. 'German-style'.

'return to nature': ironic reference to the Swiss political philosopher and writer Jean-Jacques Rousseau (1712–78), who called for an abandonment of the supposed advantages of civilization and a return to the life of the 'noble savage'.

Piedmontese: we must bear in mind that Nietzsche is writing this in Turin, the capital of the Italian region of Piedmont.

harsh judgement: a pun on the German adjective 'herb', which is also applied to wine to mean 'dry'.

21 *absurdity*: ironic allusion to the phrase *credo quia absurdum est* ('I believe because it is absurd'), attributed to the Christian Church father Tertullian (*c.*AD 155–230) as a defence of religious truth.

Schulpforta: renowned boarding-school which Nietzsche attended from 1858 to 1864. During a rebellious period in April 1863 he was punished for drinking, but thereafter was a reformed character.

In vino veritas: Lat. 'in wine lies truth', i.e. truth comes out under the influence of alcohol.

the spirit moves over water: ironic allusion to Genesis 1: 2, 'And the Spirit of God moved upon the face of the waters'.

agaçant: Fr. 'disagreeable'.

Sitting still . . . holy ghost: reference to T II 34, where Nietzsche responds to the French writer Gustave Flaubert's claim that 'One can think and write only when sitting down' with the retort: 'Only thoughts which come from *walking* have any value.'

23 *in physiologicis*: Lat. 'in physiological matters'.

24 *my Laertiana*: Nietzsche's three early (1868–70) philological essays on Diogenes Laertius (3rd. cent. AD), author of *Lives and Opinions of Eminent Philosophers*.

Sceptics: school of ancient philosophy who believed that real knowledge of things is impossible.

'largeur du coeur': Fr. 'big-heartedness'.

25 *Gyp*: Nietzsche seems to have been unaware that Gyp was a woman.

the War: the Franco-Prussian War of 1870–1.

'redeemed': Nietzsche always pokes fun at this Christian concept, especially as co-opted by Wagner in *Parsifal*, which closes with the words: 'Redemption to the Redeemer!'

25 *ex ungue Napoleonem*—: Lat. 'you may tell Napoleon from his claw'.
   Punning adaptation of the saying *ex ungue leonem* ('you may tell a lion from
   his claw'), attributed by Plutarch to the lyric poet Alcaeus of Mytilene
   (*c*.630–580 BC).

   I myself said somewhere: TI VI 8.

26 *Byron's Manfred*: eponymous, quintessentially Romantic hero of the dramatic poem first published in 1817. Byron was Nietzsche's favourite poet
   in his youth, and the inspiration for a number of his own juvenile poems
   of the early 1860s. In his December 1861 essay 'Ueber die dramatischen
   Dichtungen Byrons' ('On Byron's Dramatic Works', BAW 2: 9–15),
   Nietzsche first uses the term 'Übermensch' ('overman'), applying it precisely
   to Byron's Manfred.

   'Faust': eponymous hero of Goethe's most famous play, a two-part verse
   tragedy (1808, 1832).

   Schumann: in 1848–9 Robert Schumann composed a suite of incidental
   music to Byron's drama (Op. 115), from which the 'Manfred Overture'
   firmly established itself in the concert repertoire. Despite his criticism of
   Schumann here, Nietzsche's own piano compositions are heavily influenced
   by the composer.

   Euterpe: in Greek mythology, the muse of music. The incident referred
   to here dates back to 1872, when Nietzsche dedicated his 'Manfred
   Meditation' for piano duet to von Bülow, who was caustic in his criticism
   of the piece.

   Shakespeare . . . conceived the type of Caesar: reference to Shakespeare's
   tragedy *Julius Caesar* (1599).

   drawing on his own reality: pun on the German verb 'schöpfen', meaning
   both 'create' and 'draw' (water from a well).

   Is Hamlet understood?: development of the motif of understanding introduced in I 8. The analysis of the figure of Hamlet here reprises the discussion
   in BT 7.

   animal-self-tormentor: 'Selbstthierquäler', one of Nietzsche's more extraordinary neologisms.

   American muddle-heads and blockheads: this is the most revealing demon-
   stration of Nietzsche's subscription to the so-called 'Baconian' theory of
   Shakespeare authorship. The Americans to whom he is objecting here—
   prominent among them Delia Bacon and Ignatius Donnelly—had sought
   not to disprove the theory, but rather to prove it by the relatively pedestrian
   means of tracking down textual parallels and purportedly hidden ciphers.

   commit crime: Nietzsche is here drawing on the account of Bacon's impeach-
   ment given by Schopenhauer in *The World as Will and Representation*,
   II 19.

   the author of 'Human, All Too Human' is the visionary of 'Zarathustra': so
   different was *Human, All Too Human* from his previous works that Nietzsche

had indeed contemplated publishing it under a pseudonym ('Bernhard Cron'), before being dissuaded by his publisher.

27 *Tribschen*: small town on Lake Lucerne in central Switzerland, where Richard and Cosima Wagner lived in a spacious villa by the lakeside from March 1866 to April 1872 and were frequently visited by Nietzsche after his move to Basle in 1869.

et hoc genus omne: Lat. 'and all of this kind'.

délicatesse: Fr. 'delicacy'.

'Beyond Good and Evil', 256: in the manuscript Nietzsche inadvertently gives '256' as a page number. He is also rehearsing arguments here from *The Wagner Case*, on Wagner's 'expressivity' (cf. WC 7–9).

28 *fond*: Fr. 'foundation'.

Reich German: i.e. a supporter of the new German Empire post-1871.

Herr von Bülow: von Bülow conducted the premiere of Wagner's music drama *Tristan und Isolde* in 1865, but already in 1859 he had published a piano arrangement of the score, a copy of which was bought collectively by Nietzsche and his friends Wilhelm Pinder and Gustav Krug in spring 1861 when he was 16.

infinite: reference to Wagner's art of 'infinite melody'.

the 'Mastersingers' and the 'Ring': two of Wagner's best-known music dramas, *Die Meistersinger von Nürnberg (The Mastersingers of Nuremberg*, first performed 1868) and *Der Ring des Nibelungen (The Ring of the Nibelung*, first performed complete 1876).

29 *I myself am still enough of a Pole*: for the legend of Nietzsche's Polish extraction, cf. note on *'pur sang'*, above (p. 99).

Wagner's 'Siegfried Idyll': one of the reasons is no doubt that Nietzsche was present at its first performance, on 25 December 1870 (Cosima Wagner's birthday), at the Wagners' villa in Tribschen.

this side: again, we need to bear in mind that Nietzsche is writing in Turin.

my Venetian maestro Pietro Gasti: humorous reference to Nietzsche's friend Heinrich Köselitz (Peter Gast), who was born in Saxony but whose major composition was the comic opera *Der Löwe von Venedig (The Lion of Venice*, first performed 1891).

31 *nosce te ipsum*: 'know yourself', the proverbial Latin translation of the Greek injunction *gnothi seauton*, inscribed over the entrance to the Temple of Apollo at Delphi.

32 *egoism, self-discipline*: *'Selbstsucht, Selbstzucht'*.

33 *only just 24*: Nietzsche was indeed appointed to the chair of classical philology in Basle at this very precocious age, in the spring of 1869.

'Rheinisches Museum': Ritschl was co-editor of this academic journal, which published Nietzsche's first academic article (on the Greek poet Theognis of Megara) in March 1867, and most of his philological essays thereafter.

33 *clever Leopold von Ranke*: Ranke was born in Wiehe, roughly 30 miles west of Nietzsche's birthplace in Röcken, and was also an alumnus of Schulpforta.

German Kaiser making a pact with the Pope: Wilhelm II made the first of three visits to the Vatican in 1888.

34 *do after me—or before me*: 'mir nachmacht—oder vormacht', the latter implying 'pull the wool over my eyes'.

35 *amor fati*: Lat. 'love of fate', a crucial motif first introduced in GS 276: '*Amor fati*: let that be my love henceforth! I do not want to wage war against what is ugly. I do not want to accuse; I do not even want to accuse those who accuse. *Looking away* shall be my only negation. And all in all and on the whole: some day I wish to be only a Yes-sayer.' Cf. III 'WC' 4.

WHY I WRITE SUCH GOOD BOOKS

36 *some are born posthumously*: one of Nietzsche's most famous slogans, also used in the foreword to *The Antichrist*.

To say it again: cf. II 4.

pure folly: another reference to Wagner's *Parsifal* (cf. note to p. 17, above).

boots: taking off one's shoes as a mark of respect is a common practice in many cultures, especially out of respect for the divinity in Christianity (cf. Exodus 3: 5) and Islam. The reference to boots is presumably a dig at Nietzsche's Prussian readers.

'non legor, non legar': Lat. 'I am *not* read, I shall *not* be read'. Reworking of the phrase '*legor et legar*' ('I am read, I shall be read') from the introduction to the second edition of Schopenhauer's *Über den Willen in der Natur* (*On the Will in Nature*, 1836/1854), quoted by Nietzsche in its original form at UM III 3.

37 *'Bund'*: Bernese newspaper founded in 1850; Widmann was the reviews editor from 1880 and published his own review of *Beyond Good and Evil* in September 1886. The paper carried Spitteler's review article in January 1888.

in their own image: cf. Genesis 1: 26–7.

'overman': 'Übermensch', one of Nietzsche's key figures, who makes his first appearance in the text here. Producing the overman is the goal of the self-overcoming of humanity; he is 'beyond good and evil', the embodiment of Nietzsche's 'philosophy of the future'. Cf. III 'Z' 2, 6, 8; IV 5.

Darwinism: Nietzsche is always at pains to distance himself from Darwinism, especially 'social Darwinism', which can be summed up in the phrase 'the survival of the fittest', coined by Herbert Spencer. For Nietzsche, such a doctrine privileges the perspective of the herd.

38 *'hero cult'* . . . *reject*: again, Nietzsche frequently voices his objection to the kind of 'great men' viewed as the prime historical agents by Carlyle in his *Heroes and Hero-Worship* (1841). Cf. e.g. TI IX 12, 44; AC 54.

Parsifal: the hero of Wagner's last music drama (1882) is intended.

'Nationalzeitung' . . . 'Journal des Débats': the Berlin *National-Zeitung* was a liberal daily newspaper founded in 1848; the *Journal des Débats* was a conservative Parisian weekly newspaper originally founded in 1789 to publish the debates in the French National Assembly.

Kreuzzeitung: nickname (derived from the iron cross in its masthead) of the *Neue Preussische Zeitung*, a conservative newspaper founded in 1848.

the Poles called the French among the Slavs: for the legend of Nietzsche's Polish extraction, cf. note on *'pur sang'*, above (p. 99).

39 *romancier*: Fr. 'novelist'.

'toutes mes audaces et finesses': Fr. 'all my audacities and finesses', slightly modified quotation from a personal letter of Taine's to Nietzsche, 14 Dec. 1888.

esprit: Fr. 'wit'.

I can do no other . . . Amen: direct quotation of Martin Luther's famous words concluding his speech to the Diet of Worms in 1521.

40 *'beautiful souls'*: term from Johann Joachim Winckelmann (1717–68), German archaeologist and historian of ancient art, popularized by Goethe's novel *Wilhelm Meisters Lehrjahre* (*Wilhelm Meister's Apprenticeship*, 1795), Book VI of which is entitled 'Confessions of a Beautiful Soul'.

'feminism': *sic*. Nietzsche's preferred term, a French loan-word.

searchers, tempters, experimenters: 'Suchern, Versuchern', a favourite pun of Nietzsche's. The passage is a direct quotation from Z III, 'On the Vision and the Riddle', 1.

grope . . . with cowardly hand: allusion to Theseus's escape from the labyrinth after killing the Minotaur in Greek mythology, aided by a ball of thread given to him by Ariadne.

41 *pure folly*: another reference to Wagner's *Parsifal* (cf. note to p. 17, above). The context here is an attack on the Kantian notion of the 'thing in itself'.

superhuman: 'übermenschlich', i.e. pertaining to the overman.

commonly agreed . . . common or garden philosophers: pun on 'alle Welt' ('the whole world') and 'Allerweltsphilosophen' ('unexceptional philosophers').

hollow-pots, cabbage-heads: another pun in German ('Hohltöpfe, Kohlköpfe').

42 *Circe*: enchantress in Homer's *Odyssey*.

psychologica: Lat. 'psychological matters'.

eternal feminine: term frequently adopted by Nietzsche from the words of the 'Chorus Mysticus' at the conclusion of Goethe's *Faust, Part Two* (1832), 'The eternal feminine | Draws us on'.

maenads: female worshippers of Dionysus in Greek mythology, noted for their wild, drunken behaviour and responsible, *inter alia*, for the violent deaths of Pentheus and Orpheus.

42 *'beautiful souls'*: cf. note to p. 40, above.

   Love . . . deadly hatred of the sexes: quotation from WC 2.

   thus spoke Zarathustra: not an actual quotation from Nietzsche's earlier book, although Zarathustra is perfectly capable of expressing such sentiments. Cf., for example, the passage in Z I, 'On Reading and Writing', quoted as the epigraph to the Third Essay of *On the Genealogy of Morals*: 'Courageous, untroubled, mocking, violent—thus does Wisdom want us: she is a woman and always loves only a warrior.'

43 *'idealist' of a woman*: allusion to Nietzsche's friend Malwida von Meysenbug (1816–1903), author of the autobiographical *Memoiren einer Idealistin* (*Memoirs of an Idealist*, 3 vols., 1869–76).

   anti-nature: 'Widernatur', Nietzsche's neologism for 'perversity' (the usual word is 'Widernatürlichkeit'). Cf. IV 7 and TI V.

   'preaching chastity . . . holy spirit of life': quotation from the short text 'Law against Christianity' which Nietzsche wrote on 30 September 1888 and eventually intended to use as a conclusion to *The Antichrist*.

44 *'The genius of the heart . . . back-streaming . . .'*: slightly repunctuated quotation from BGE 295, the penultimate numbered paragraph in the book. The object of the description is presumably Nietzsche himself.

The Birth of Tragedy

45 *Parsifal*: Wagner's last music drama was premiered at the second Bayreuth Festival in 1882, a decade after Nietzsche published *The Birth of Tragedy*.

   Hellenism and Pessimism . . . more unambiguous title: this was indeed the subtitle Nietzsche gave to the second edition of the text in 1886.

   Schopenhauer . . . wrong about everything: cf. section 6 of the 'Attempt at a Self-Criticism' with which Nietzsche prefaced the second edition of the text.

   Battle of Woerth: one of the early engagements in the Franco-Prussian War, fought on 6 August 1870.

   sublated to become a unity: Nietzsche here uses the Hegelian term 'aufgehoben', which simultaneously conveys the senses 'raised', 'preserved', and 'cancelled out'.

   Opera . . . and revolution: allusion to Wagner's 1849 pamphlet *Kunst und Revolution* (*Art and Revolution*).

46 *'Rationality' . . . life-undermining power!*: Nietzsche's arguments against Socrates are laid out in more detail in TI II.

   At one point . . . 'subterraneans': paraphrase of the end of BT 24.

   I was the first . . . the Dionysian: Nietzsche makes a similar claim at TI X 4.

47 *to sanction, to call 'good'*: a pun in the German, on 'gutheissen' ('sanction') and 'gut heissen' ('call good').

Aristotle's misunderstanding of it: reference to Aristotle's main comments on tragic drama in the *Poetics*, specifically the concept of *catharsis* (*Poetics*, VI, 1449b).

'Saying yes to life . . . the joy of destruction': slightly modified quotation from TI X 5.

great philosophical Greeks . . . before Socrates: i.e. the 'pre-Socratic' philosophers whom Nietzsche particularly prized. See e.g. *Philosophy in the Tragic Age of the Greeks* (1873).

48 *the Stoics . . . show traces of it*: the Stoic philosophers themselves viewed Heraclitus as a precursor and adopted his cosmology, in particular.

'Wagner in Bayreuth': *Richard Wagner in Bayreuth* (1876), the fourth of Nietzsche's *Untimely Meditations*.

49 *great noon-day*: phrase used repeatedly in *Thus Spoke Zarathustra* to designate the impending crisis of man's self-overcoming. Cf. Z I, 'On the Bestowing Virtue', 3, and III 'D' 2.

page 7: the page reference is to the first edition of *Richard Wagner in Bayreuth* (corresponding to UM IV 1).

fata morgana: Lat. 'mirage'.

Anti-Alexanders . . . undone: reference to a legend associated with Alexander the Great, who purportedly sliced through this particularly convoluted knot with his sword in 333 BC.

on page 30: passage corresponding to the end of UM IV 4.

page 71: passage corresponding to the beginning of UM IV 9.

pages 43–6: passage corresponding to UM IV 6.

The Untimelies

50 *'Untimelies'*: abbreviation for *Untimely Meditations* (*Unzeitgemässe Betrachtungen*, 1873–6), also translated as 'Thoughts out of Season', 'Unmodern Observations', and 'Unfashionable Observations'.

first attack (1873): David Strauss, the Confessor and the Writer.

second 'Untimely' (1874): On the Uses and Disadvantages of History for Life.

third and fourth 'Untimelies': respectively, *Schopenhauer as Educator* (1874) and *Richard Wagner in Bayreuth* (1876).

egoism, self-discipline: '*Selbstsucht, Selbstzucht*' again; cf. II 9.

51 *'old faith and the new'*: the title of the book by Strauss that is the main object of Nietzsche's attack.

entered the language through my essay: not quite true, since it had been used earlier by Nietzsche's Basle colleague Gustav Teichmüller (who also pre-empted his use of the term 'perspectivism'), although it has been regarded as Nietzsche's coinage ever since.

51 *'Prussian blue'*: dark-blue pigment used in paints and (formerly) blueprints; one of the oldest known synthetic compounds.

infamous 'Grenzboten': *Die Grenzboten* was a national-liberal newspaper founded in Brussels in 1841 for German political exiles, published from 1843 in Leipzig. In October 1873 it published a review by 'B.F.' entitled 'Herr Friedrich Nietzsche und die deutsche Cultur' ('Mr Friedrich Nietzsche and German Culture').

the death of Strauss: Strauss did indeed die in 1874, soon after Nietzsche's polemic appeared.

old Hegelian Bruno Bauer: ironic reference to one of the most prominent erstwhile members of the 'Young Hegelians'.

Karl Hillebrand . . . collected writings: Hillebrand's review 'Nietzsche gegen Strauss' ('Nietzsche contra Strauss') was first published in the *Augsburger Zeitung* in September 1873. In the end he published three separate reviews on the first three of Nietzsche's *Untimely Meditations*.

52 *playing the purists*: German language purism achieved public popularity again at the end of the nineteenth century, as evidenced by the founding of the Allgemeiner Deutscher Sprachverein ('General German Language Society') in 1885 and its journal *Muttersprache* ('*Mother Tongue*') the following year.

one of Stendhal's maxims: reported by Prosper Mérimée in his introduction to Stendhal's *Correspondance inédite* (1855).

'libres penseurs': Fr. 'free-thinkers'. Nietzsche is generally critical of such people, preferring to associate with 'free spirits' ('freier Geister').

53 *on p. 93*: passage to be found towards the end of UM III 7.

I could see the land: Nietzsche takes up the biblical motif of the 'promised land' here, as in the preface to *On the Genealogy of Morals*. Cf. also GS 382, quoted at III 'Z' 2.

the philosopher . . . puts everything in danger: pre-empts Nietzsche's famous claim at IV 1, 'I am not a man, I am dynamite'. Cf. also TI IX 44.

Human, All Too Human

55 *a book for free spirits*: the book's subtitle.

hundredth anniversary . . . 1878: the first edition of the book bore a dedication to the memory of Voltaire.

grandseigneur: Fr. 'overlord'.

56 *the first Bayreuth Festival*: held in the summer of 1876. Nietzsche attended a week of rehearsals at the end of July before succumbing to psychosomatic illness and fleeing to the Bavarian Forest, from where he was coaxed back to Bayreuth by his sister in time to attend the whole of the first performance of the *Ring* cycle in mid-August.

the laying of the foundation stone: a ceremony Nietzsche attended in 1872.

'Bayreuther Blätter': the Wagnerians' 'house journal', published monthly by the Allgemeiner Richard-Wagner-Verein ('General Richard Wagner Society') from January 1878 (cf. III 'HA' 5).

A kingdom for one sensible word!: reworked quotation from Shakespeare's *Richard III*, Act V, Scene 4.

with grace ad infinitum: ironic allusion to the Three Graces of Greek mythology.

gone among swine: allusion to the New Testament episode of Jesus casting out devils into the Gadarene swine. Cf. Matthew 8: 32; Mark 5: 13; Luke 8: 33.

charming Parisian woman: Louise Ott, friend of Nietzsche's.

57 *'profession'. . . last of all*: pun on 'Beruf' ('profession', 'calling') and 'berufen' ('to appoint', 'to call', 'to summon').

59 *one very explicit passage*: HA I 37, quoted more or less verbatim in what follows.

60 *lisez*: Fr. 'for which read' (1888 interpolation).

Daybreak

61 *Thoughts on Morality as Prejudice*: Nietzsche misquotes himself here. The actual subtitle is 'Thoughts on the Prejudices of Morality'.

like a conclusion, not like a cannon shot: pun on 'Schluss' ('conclusion') and 'Schuss' ('shot').

young Greek god . . . little lizard: reference to one of the most famous representations of Apollo, by the Greek sculptor Praxiteles. Known as *Apollo Sauroktonos* ('Apollo the Lizard-Slayer'), it depicted the young god leaning against a tree and holding an arrow, with which he was about to spear a lizard crawling up towards him.

'There are so many dawns that have not yet broken': epigraph taken from the Hindu religious text the *Rigveda*.

morality of unselfing oneself: 'Entselbstungs-Moral', a striking new compound noun.

The Gay Science

64 *'la gaya scienza'*: Provençal term for poetry, used by Nietzsche as the subtitle to his book.

You who . . . Fairest Januarius!: verbatim quotation of the verse motto to Book IV of *The Gay Science* (1882).

at the conclusion of the fourth book: the final section in Book IV (GS 342), which originally brought the book to its conclusion (until Nietzsche added Book V for the second edition in 1887), introduces the figure of Zarathustra and is subsequently reused almost verbatim at the start of *Thus Spoke Zarathustra*, for which it acts as a 'trailer'.

Thus Spoke Zarathustra

65 *Lake Silvaplana*: near Sils-Maria in the Upper Engadine.

when Richard Wagner died in Venice: on 13 February 1883.

65 *the opening of 'Zarathustra' itself*: cf. note to p. 64, above.

penultimate section of the fourth book: GS 341, 'The Greatest Weight'.

66 *Lou von Salomé*: notoriously, Nietzsche wanted to become more than just 'friendly' with Lou and proposed marriage to her in 1882 (via Paul Rée), but was rebuffed.

albergo: It. 'inn'.

Friedrich III: who had recently died, in June 1888.

67 *Argonauts*: in Greek mythology, a group of heroes who sailed aboard Jason's ship the *Argo* in search of the Golden Fleece.

68 *'We who are new . . . the tragedy begins . . .'*: a few minor modifications aside, Nietzsche here reproduces the whole of GS 382, 'Great Health'. The concluding words echo the title of paragraph 342 (the final paragraph in the first edition of *The Gay Science*), 'Incipit tragoedia'.

being-outside-yourself: 'Ausser-sich-sein', a formulation which recalls the portrayal of Dionysian 'ecstasy' in BT 1.

69 *'here all things . . . how to talk'*: slightly modified quotation from Z III, 'The Return Home'.

comme il faut: Fr. 'as is right and proper'.

Aquila . . . Friedrich II: Friedrich II founded this city in central Italy in the mid-thirteenth century as a defence against the spread of papal power. The etymology of the place-name ('Eagle', derived from the Hohenstaufen coat-of-arms) doubtless also appealed to Nietzsche.

Palazzo del Quirinale: the Quirinal Palace—formerly a papal residence, from 1871 the official royal residence of the kings of Italy, since 1946 the residence of the Italian president.

'Night-Song': in Z II.

70 *third and last part*: Nietzsche here deliberately passes over in silence the problematic Part IV (1885), which had such limited distribution that he can assume it will not be familiar to his present readers.

'On Old and New Tablets': in Z III.

I could often be seen dancing: an ironic comment in the light of the incident which took place shortly before Nietzsche's breakdown, a few weeks after he wrote this, when he was observed by his landlady singing and dancing naked in his room.

rancune: Fr. 'grudge', 'rancour'.

71 *Veda*: large series of Hindu religious texts from ancient India.

'I draw circles . . . sacred mountains': quotation from Z III, 'On Old and New Tablets', 19.

72 *what is truth*: allusion to the other most famous quotation from Pontius Pilate in the Bible, his question to Jesus reported at John 18: 38.

soul-study: 'Seelen-Erforschung', a passable gloss on 'psychology'.

return . . . figurativeness: another allusion to Rousseau's notion of a 'return to nature' (cf. note to p. 20, above).

73 *the soul . . . ebb and flood*: slightly modified quotation from Z III, 'On Old and New Tablets', 19.

'*the enormous and unbounded Yea- and Amen-saying*': quotation from Z III, 'Before the Sunrise', itself an allusion to 2 Corinthians 1: 20.

'*Into all abysses I carry my blessing Yea-saying*': another quotation (this time slightly modified) from Z III, 'Before the Sunrise'.

75 *Night it is . . . the song of a lover—*: a few minor modifications aside, Nietzsche here reproduces the whole of the ninth chapter of Part II of *Thus Spoke Zarathustra*.

Ariadne: in Greek mythology, Bacchus (Dionysus) successfully woos Ariadne on the island of Naxos after she has been abandoned there by her former lover Theseus.

76 *I walk . . . redemption*: slightly modified quotation from Z II, 'On Redemption'.

great disgust at man: cf. Z II, 'On the Rabble', quoted in I 8.

Willing-no-more . . . the Gods to me now! . . .: slightly modified quotation from the conclusion of Z II, 'Upon the Isles of the Blest'.

'*Become hard!*': quotation from Z III, 'On Old and New Tablets', 29, used again as the conclusion to *Twilight of the Idols*.

Beyond Good and Evil

77 *gentilhomme*: Fr. 'gentleman'.

you mustn't have learnt to fear: describes Wagner's heroic character Siegfried, as portrayed in the third music drama of the *Ring* cycle.

petits faits: Fr. 'small facts'.

the Tsar: Alexander III of Russia (reigned 1881–94). In German there is a perfect assonance between 'Tsar' and 'Zarathustra'.

78 *God being idle on that seventh day*: cf. the description of the origin of the Sabbath in Genesis 2: 2.

Genealogy of Morals

79 *Genealogy of Morals*: another slightly truncated title, omitting 'On the' ('Zur').

tempo feroce: It. 'fierce tempo'.

'*For man . . . not will*': slight misquotation of the book's concluding words (GM III 28; cf. GM III 1).

Twilight of the Idols

80 *All 'dark stress' . . . the right way*: allusion to Goethe's *Faust, Part One*, ll. 328–9: 'A good man, in his dark, bewildered stress,|Well knows the path from which he should not stray.' The words are spoken by God

towards the end of the 'Prologue in Heaven' (here quoted in the translation by David Luke).

81 *the 'Revaluation'*: i.e. *The Antichrist*.

The Wagner Case

82 *ridendo dicere severum*: Lat. 'through what is laughable say what is sombre', the motto of the book and a variation on *ridentem dicere verum, quid vetat* ('What forbids us to tell the truth, laughing?') by the Roman poet Horace (*Satires*, I. 24).

verum dicere: Lat. 'saying what is true'.

évangile des humbles: Fr. 'gospel of the humble', description of Christianity by the French writer Ernest Renan (1823–92).

the Trumpeter of Säckingen: eponymous hero of a popular opera (1884) by the German composer Victor Nessler (1841–90).

83 *Liszt Association . . . wily church music*: pun on the composer's name and the adjective 'listig' ('cunning', 'wily').

in historicis: Lat. 'in historical matters'.

'Deutschland, Deutschland über Alles': 'Germany, Germany above all', first line of the 'Lied der Deutschen' ('Song of the Germans', 1841) by the German poet Heinrich Hoffmann von Fallersleben (1798–1874), adopted as the German national anthem in 1922.

imperium romanum: Lat. 'Roman empire'.

'categorical imperative': Kant's basis of all moral action as developed in the *Kritik der praktischen Vernunft* (*Critique of Practical Reason*, 1788) and first formulated in the *Grundlegung zur Metaphysik der Sitten* (*Groundwork of the Metaphysics of Morals*, 1785): 'Act only on that maxim which you can at the same time will to become a universal law.'

84 *'Wars of Liberation'*: collective term applied to the successful campaign (1813–15) fought by the Prussian armies (in alliance with those of the Russian tsar) against the forces of Napoleon.

névrose nationale: Fr. 'national neurosis'.

labour . . . mouse: allusion to Horace's saying 'Mountains will go into labour, and a silly little mouse will be born' (*Ars Poetica*, l. 139).

85 *veil-makers*: the original meaning of the surname 'Schleiermacher'.

in psychologicis: Lat. 'in psychological matters'.

A German . . . shallow: cf. TI I 27.

86 *third 'Untimely', p. 71*: passage corresponding to UM III 6, written and published in 1874 when Nietzsche was 30, so '26' is an error.

saviour of the Capitol: i.e. 'goose', in allusion to the legend that when the Gauls of Brennus besieged Rome in 390 BC, the Capitoline Hill was saved from sacking by the cackling of the sacred geese.

un-beautiful soul: cf. note to p. 40, above.

délicatesse: Fr. 'delicacy'.

87 *Ten years*: i.e. since Nietzsche alienated most of his friends by publishing *Human, All Too Human* in 1878.

I sent 'The Wagner Case' out into the world: not only an allusion to the practice, customary since classical times, of referring to literary works as emissaries with their own fate, but also a reminder that the literary form of *The Wagner Case* is that of an open letter.

immortalize themselves!: pun on the adverb 'unsterblich', meaning both 'utterly' and 'immortally'.

WHY I AM A DESTINY

88 *I am not a man, I am dynamite*: Nietzsche is actually quoting here, from Widmann's review of *Beyond Good and Evil* in September 1886 (cf. note to p. 37, above). Dynamite was a relatively recent invention, patented by Alfred Nobel only in 1867.

become flesh: allusion to John 1: 14: 'And the word was made flesh.'

removal of mountain and valley: Cf. Z II, 'The Stillest Hour': '"Oh Zarathustra, whoever has to move mountains also moves valleys and lowlands".' Both passages allude to 1 Corinthians 13: 2 (cf. Matthew 17: 20, 21: 21; Mark 11: 23).

89 *which becomes man*: another biblical motif, describing Jesus as the divine human.

And whoever . . . the creative: slightly modified quotation from Z II, 'On Self-Overcoming'.

90 *Persian virtue*: cf. Z I, 'On the Thousand and One Goals'. Allusion to the description of the Persians by the Greek historian Herodotus: 'They educate boys from 5 years old until they are 20 in three things only: horsemanship, archery, and to be truthful' (*Histories*, I. 136).

niaiserie: Fr. 'foolishness'.

91 *homines optimi*: Lat. 'best of men'.

good men . . . the good: slightly modified quotation from Z III, 'On Old and New Tablets', 7 and 28.

The good . . . most harmful harm: slightly modified quotation from Z III, 'On Old and New Tablets', 26.

92 *'On which distant futures . . .'*: this and the following are direct quotations from Z II, 'On Human Cleverness'.

93 *Disgust at man is my danger*: cf. I 8 and III 'Z' 8.

anti-nature: cf. note to p. 43, above.

categorical imperative: cf. note to p. 83, above.

94 *the revaluation . . . hostile to life*: Nietzsche's 'revaluation', in other words, turns 'topsy-turvy' values the right way up again. Cf. the foreword to *Twilight of the Idols*.

94 *idiosyncrasy*: the primary sense here is medico-physiological ('physical constitution peculiar to a person').

95 *Morality as vampirism*: a striking image, first deployed in GS 372.

folie circulaire: Fr. 'intermittent madness', now known as 'manic-depressive illness' or 'bipolar disorder'.

Écrasez l'infâme!: Fr. 'Crush the infamy!', Voltaire's motto in his fight against Christianity.

GLOSSARY OF NAMES

Alexander the Great (356–323 BC) king of Macedon, legendary military leader, and pupil of Aristotle

Aristotle (384–322 BC) Greek philosopher

Baader, Franz Xaver von (1765–1841) German philosopher and theologian

Bach, Johann Sebastian (1685–1750) German Baroque composer

Bacon, Sir Francis, Viscount St Alban (1561–1626) English philosopher, essayist, and statesman

Baudelaire, Charles (1821–67) French 'Decadent' poet, critic, and translator

Bauer, Bruno (1809–82) German philosopher, historian, and theologian; leader of the Hegelian left in the 1840s

Berlioz, Hector (1803–69) French Romantic composer

Bismarck, Otto von (1815–98) German statesman, the leading political figure of Nietzsche's time

Borgia, Cesare (1474/6–1507) Italian general, cardinal, and political machinator

Bourget, Paul (1852–1935) French novelist and cultural critic

Brandes, Georg (1842–1927) Danish scholar and critic

Brendel, Karl Franz (1811–68) German musicologist and composer

Brochard, Victor (1848–1907) French philosopher

Buddha (Siddhartha Gautama, c.563–483 BC) Nepalese spiritual leader, founder of Buddhism

Bülow, Hans von (1830–94) German conductor, pianist, and composer; first husband of Cosima Wagner and a champion of Richard Wagner's music

Byron, Lord (George Gordon Noel, 1788–1824) English Romantic poet and satirist

Caesar, Julius (100–44 BC) Roman emperor and general

Cagliostro, Count Alessandro di (Giuseppe Balsamo, 1743–95) Italian adventurer, occultist, forger, and Freemason

Carlyle, Thomas (1795–1881) Scottish writer and literary historian

Chopin, Frédéric (1810–49) Polish pianist-composer

Claude Lorrain (Claude Gellée, 1600–82) French Baroque landscape painter

Corneille, Pierre (1606–84) French tragic dramatist

Dante Alighieri (1265–1321) Italy's national poet, author of the *Divine Comedy*

Darwin, Charles (1809–82) English natural historian, proponent of the theory of evolution by 'natural selection'

Delacroix, Eugène (1798–1863) French Romantic painter

Descartes, René (1596–1650) French rationalist philosopher, mathematician, and scientist

Dühring, Eugen (1833–1921) German socialist philosopher and economist

Ewald, Heinrich Georg August (1803–75) German theologian and orientalist

Fichte, Johann Gottlieb (1762–1814) German idealist philosopher

Förster-Nietzsche, Elisabeth (1846–1935) the philosopher's sister

France, Anatole (Jacques Anatole François Thibault, 1844–1924) French writer, awarded the Nobel Prize for Literature in 1921

Friedrich II (1194–1250) Holy Roman Emperor from 1220 till his death

Friedrich III (1831–88) German emperor and king of Prussia for ninety-nine days in 1888, between Wilhelm I and Wilhelm II (q.v.)

Fritzsch, Ernst Wilhelm (1840–1902) Leipzig-based German publisher

Gast, Peter (Heinrich Köselitz, 1854–1918) German composer and writer, Nietzsche's friend and amanuensis

Goethe, Johann Wolfgang von (1749–1832) Germany's national poet

Gyp (Sibylle-Gabrielle Marie-Antoinette de Riquetti de Mirabeau, Comtesse de Martel de Janville, 1849–1932) French writer

Handel, George Frideric (1685–1759) German-born Baroque composer

Hegel, Georg Wilhelm Friedrich (1770–1831) German idealist philosopher

Heine, Heinrich (1797–1856) German poet and critic

Heraclitus of Ephesus (*c.*550–480 BC) Greek pre-Socratic philosopher, who held that 'all things are in flux'

Herder, Johann Gottfried (1744–1803) German critic, writer on aesthetics, philosophy, and theology

Hillebrand, Karl (1829–84) German essayist and historian

Hoffmann, Franz (1804–81) German philosopher

Horace (Quintus Horatius Flaccus, 65–8 BC) Roman poet

Ibsen, Henrik (1828–1906) Norwegian Naturalist dramatist

Kant, Immanuel (1724–1804) German Enlightenment philosopher

Kohl, Johann Georg (1808–78) German geographer, cartographer, and writer

La Rochefoucauld, François duc de (1613–80) French *moraliste* and aphorist

Leibniz, Gottfried Wilhelm (1646–1716) German rationalist philosopher, mathematician, and polymath

Lemaitre, Jules (1853–1914) French dramatist and critic

Leonardo da Vinci (1452–1519) Italian Renaissance painter and polymath

Liszt, Franz (1811–86) Hungarian pianist-composer (and Richard Wagner's father-in-law)

Loti, Pierre (Louis-Marie-Julien Viaud, 1850–1923) French writer and naval officer

Luther, Martin (1483–1546) German religious reformer and Bible translator

Maupassant, Guy de (1850–93) French novelist and short-story writer

Meilhac, Henri (1831–97) French dramatist and librettist

Mérimée, Prosper (1803–70) French short-story writer, novelist, and dramatist

Molière (Jean-Baptiste Poquelin, 1622–73) French comic dramatist

Montaigne, Michel Eyquem de (1533–92) French essayist

Napoleon Bonaparte (1769–1821) French emperor (1804–14) and general

Nietzsche, Carl Ludwig (1813–49) the philosopher's father

Nietzsche, Franziska, née Oehler (1826–97) the philosopher's mother

Nohl, Ludwig (1831–85) German musicologist, biographer of Wagner

Pascal, Blaise (1623–62) French mathematician and religious philosopher

Plato (428–347 BC) Greek philosopher; pupil of Socrates, founder of the Athenian Academy, and writer of philosophical dialogues

Pohl, Richard (1826–96) German music critic

Racine, Jean (1639–99) French tragic dramatist

Ranke, Leopold von (1795–1866) German historian

Rée, Paul (1849–1901) German philosopher and physician, Nietzsche's friend

Ritschl, Friedrich Wilhelm (1806–76) German classicist, Nietzsche's teacher

Rossini, Gioacchino (1792–1868) Italian composer

Sallust (Gaius Sallustius Crispus, 86–35 BC) Roman writer and historian

Salomé, Lou von (1861–1937) Russian-born writer and psychoanalyst, Nietzsche's friend

Schelling, Friedrich Wilhelm Joseph von (1775–1854) German idealist philosopher

Schleiermacher, Friedrich Daniel Ernst (1768–1834) German theologian and philosopher

Schopenhauer, Arthur (1788–1860) German philosopher, Nietzsche's early mentor

Schumann, Robert (1810–56) German Romantic composer

Schütz, Heinrich (1585–1672) German early Baroque composer

Shakespeare, William (1564–1616) English national poet and dramatist

Socrates (*c.*470–399 BC) Greek philosopher, generally accepted as the founding father of the Western intellectual tradition

Spencer, Herbert (1820–1903) English philosopher and sociologist, proponent of 'social Darwinism'

Spitteler, Carl Friedrich Georg (1845–1924) Swiss-German poet, awarded the Nobel Prize for Literature in 1919

Stein, Heinrich von (1857–87) German philosopher and writer, disciple of Wagner

Stendhal (Henri Beyle, 1783–1842) French novelist

Strauss, David Friedrich (1808–74) German theologian and writer

Taine, Hippolyte (1828–93) French historian

Treitschke, Heinrich von (1834–96) German historian and political writer

Vischer, Friedrich Theodor (1807–87) German aesthetician

Vittorio Emanuele II (1820–78) first king of the united Italy from 1861 till his death

Voltaire (François-Marie Arouet, 1694–1778) French Enlightenment philosopher and writer

Wagner, Cosima (1837–1930) Italian-born daughter of Franz Liszt, wife of Hans von Bülow then of Richard Wagner (qq.v.)

Wagner, Richard (1813–83) German Romantic composer, Nietzsche's early mentor and later antagonist

Widmann, Joseph Viktor (1842–1911) Swiss-German writer and journalist

Wilhelm II (1859–1941) last German emperor and king of Prussia, 1888–1918

Zoroaster ('Zarathustra', 6th century BC?) ancient Iranian prophet and religious teacher, founder of Zoroastrianism

INDEX

For ease of use, cross-references within major semantic fields have been grouped under the following entries: animal; art(ist); body; economy; education; fate(ful); food; happiness; light; music; politics; power(ful); religion; rhetoric; sick(ness); time; war; weather; writing.